THE CIVILIAN'S SOUTH INDIA

THE CIVILIAN'S SOUTH INDIA

SOME PLACES AND PEOPLE IN MADRAS

"CIVILIAN"

GYAN

Published by

Gyan Publishing House
5, Ansari Road
Daryaganj, New Delhi-110002
Phone: 011-47034999, 9811692060
E-mail: books@gyanbooks.com

Distribution Network
gyanbooks.com
India, USA, Canada, UK, Australia, France

ISBN : 978-81-212-3247-0 (PB)
First Published, London, 1921

2nd Impression 2020

Printed at: Gyan Press, Delhi.

Civilian's South India

THE CIVILIAN'S SOUTH INDIA

SOME PLACES AND PEOPLE IN MADRAS

BY "CIVILIAN"

JOHN LANE, THE BODLEY HEAD, LIMITED
LONDON MCMXXI

CONTENTS

FOREWORD

WHEN the Civilian, being then of nearly four years' standing, suggested to his Superior that it was high time he should write something about India, his Superior was not encouraging.

" Do you mean to say," he remarked, " that you contemplate the crime of publishing ? "

The Civilian pointed out that he had previously on some one or two occasions been guilty of that same offence.

" Then," said the Superior, " do not do so any more. Give it up. It is neither decent, nor *mamul*, nor anything else that is good. And, moreover, enough has been written about India already."

" Not about South India," said the Civilian, " and I really think it is high time people at home realized that there are other parts of India besides the Punjab."

The Superior shrugged his shoulders and asked what the Civilian knew about India. The Civilian replied that in very truth he knew nothing, but that it was his firm belief that no one ever would know anything or ever had, and that therefore one might as well set down one's impressions. By now his impressions might be said to have taken shape, their crudities to have worn off.

"I do not, for instance," he said, "dislike you so heartily as I should have done three years ago, because I can now see your good points; certain mannerisms of the Indian no longer make me feel uncomfortable because I realize that by them he means no harm; I do not feel this country so abominably hot because I have become used to it. In a few years, on the other hand, I shall have become so used to it that I shall see or notice nothing at all. The hour therefore seems ripe."

"You are talking like a fool," said his Superior.

"Nevertheless," said the Civilian, "I mean to do it."

PART I

PLACES

THE CIVILIAN'S SOUTH INDIA

I

THE EDGE OF INDIA

TO India, if one has once made up one's mind, there are ways and ways of going. In all the books the Civilian ever read the hero and the heroine and all their people travelled by a line of steamboats known as the P. and O., and were disembarked in due and proper form at Bombay. Thence they wandered away to places in the North of India, where from all accounts they led strange and extravagant lives. The hero at once became entangled with luscious Eurasian ladies, while the heroine complicated the situation by attaching herself to Ruling Princes of any kind or character which happened to suit the novelist for the time being. Now the Civilian —he admits it with a sort of regret—has never been entangled with Eurasian ladies, and he never even set eyes on a Ruling Prince. His life, indeed, has been singularly devoid so far of adventure of any sort; and he thinks this must be due to the fact that he did not in the first instance do the thing properly and come out by Bombay and the P. and O. Being an indirect and muddling sort of creature, he came to India by Ceylon.

The Civilian, you see, was going to Madras, a thing which Heroes and Heroines do not seem to go in for. When the lady-relatives of the Civilian heard that he was posted to Madras, they wept. "There is something," they said, "about a Madras Civilian—— " and no doubt they were right. They urged him to apply for a transfer; but even at that early age the Civilian had sense enough to realize the methods of Government with such as apply for transfers. They would probably have put him in the Tower. So he bought a set of Kipling's works instead; but that did him little good either, for he learned from these that Madras was the Benighted Presidency, the fossilized remains of a place rather than a place itself; and *William the Conqueror*—who you will remember did Famine Relief work there—told him it was a place to be avoided by all right-thinking people. (He subsequently learned that *William* and her friends were a somewhat ill-informed lot, more especially on the subjects of the Madras Presidency and Famine Relief; but he did not know that at the time.) He was just becoming really depressed when he met a man in a public-house called the *Duke of Portland* in the Euston Road. The man was a newspaper man and he had a nice rosy face, and he was eating a very fine lunch and seemed quite pleased with himself altogether. "Madras?" he said. "I was thirty-five years in Madras. Feel that muscle." There was nothing at all wrong with the muscle. Subsequently they drank beer together, and the Civilian thought that if it contained such men as this Madras might be indeed Benighted, but scarcely fossilized. He decided, however, that it was a place to be approached warily, so he crept round its tail, as it were, and stalked it from Ceylon. Much as a geologist, seeing a fossilized ichthyosaurus on the opposite hillside, might yet creep at it round the head of the valley for fear it might after all come to life.

The Fable of the Civilian and the Hearty Editor is introduced to point the obvious moral that it is better in most cases to trust the man who has been to see. It is also introduced because the Civilian wishes to observe that there is an exception to this rule and that that exception arises in the case of India. It is no good asking people about India even if they have been there: either they know nothing about it or they tell you deliberate lies. The Civilian once wanted to know about a small place in India, so he asked two men, one of whom had spent six years there and the other three. The first said it was so consistently warm that one was never able to wear long pyjamas, that the wind always blew off the landward hills, and that you had to remain in headquarters three months of the year because of rain. The second said that one required an overcoat from October onwards, that there was always a fine sea breeze, and that it never rained at all. Being inexperienced, the Civilian went to take the casting vote of a third man who had never been in the place but had lived a long time within sixty miles of it, and *he* said quite promptly and decidedly that the place did not exist. The Civilian found this with all subjects on which he asked questions, and he eventually formulated a theory that the gods of India, for their sport, foist various hallucinations upon the several Europeans sojourning in their territory. Perhaps no European has ever seen India at all. At any rate it seems perfectly clear —this is important, and the Civilian begs you to realize and assimilate it *ab initio*—that what you will read here will be no more than the hallucinations to which the gods of India have chosen to subject the Civilian.

There was a clever young man going out on the Civilian's boat who made an epigram after lunch on "The glory that's the East and the glamour that's—Port Said." It is perhaps necessary to point out that he meant this as a parody of "The glory that was Greece and the grandeur that was Rome"—lines which, like most people, he wrongly attributed to Byron. It was a shocking bad parody, but the clever young man had got hold of a great truth. It is only permissible to refer to the "glamour of the East" so long as you make it quite clear that you exempt India.

Port Said is still in some aspects an offensive place—but it does convey a certain sense of flashy and mysterious magnificence, which is what the Civilian understands by glamour. He has been told, too, that if you continue very much further east, you will come on the same thing again in

Canton and some of the China ports. In the intervening region it does not exist. There is a bright prettiness about Ceylon, and Burma is in places highly-coloured, but they possess no glamour. India possesses almost everything else, but the "glamour of the East," which lady novelists make their heroines experience going along in the train—in Indian trains of all places—it has not. If you have any doubts on this subject, come and live in it for a year. What the clever young man meant by "the glory that's the East" he probably could not have told you; nor can the Civilian, but he has a feeling that it did express a certain truth. That truth, the Civilian fancies, is going to be the first of many things he will find himself unable to express on paper, and so he will not make the attempt. Let it stand as the clever young man said it; at all events it pleased himself and his hearers at the time, which is always something.

Colombo—or that part of it which the shore-going Ulysses sees—is not really a town; it is a passenger-ship, a Bibby liner or maybe an Orient, which has moored there and fossilized. At the bow is the *G.O.H.*—the *Grand Oriental Hotel*, that is, where they make the best cider cup in Asia—and at the stern, standing out into the sea, is the *Galle Face* ("Gaul," please, not "Galley"). Along the decks instead of cabins there are wonderful shops selling moonstones and carved elephants and Burmese silks and swami silverwork, and all at three to ten times the proper price. All the people one meets on Bibby and City and Orient boats go to and fro along this deck; and the good *G.O.H.* is the smoking-room and the Ladies' Drawing-Room is the *Galle Face*. The only thing which mars the ship illusion is that right amidships there is a lighthouse, which is scarcely usual; otherwise it is perfect. Instead of ship's officers there appear from time to time tearing young men on motor cycles who incite you to drink—cocktails, too, in a soaking damp heat somewhere about ninety. The Civilian thought they were killing themselves, but not they. If you follow the dust of their motor cycles, however, you will get away from the ship and come to the real Colombo—a vast place of parks and palm avenues and endless little cigar-box bungalows. There is a sense of infinity about it—and of pleasaunce. You remember that new kingdom the Argonauts found on their homeward way to Iolcos—a kingdom of merchant princes doing themselves exceedingly well? That was an earlier version of Colombo; and Ceylon, as the Civilian saw it, was almost all like that.

"But," will say the Superior at this stage, "you said you were going to write about India. Why waste our time in Ceylon—of which you can know absolutely nothing?" Well, there *is* a reason and the Civilian will state it. It is because he desires to warn all persons proceeding to India for a period of years not on any account, as they value their peace of mind, to go by way of Ceylon. It will unsettle their intellects, it will upset all their standards, it will lead them to entirely false expectations. "If this is India," they shall say, "this is all right." If it were it would be; but, alas, alas, it is not! Ceylon is a merry island; it is pretty and pleasant and playful; it is innocuous, it is controlled, it is cultivated and laid-out and safe; it is the island of the smiling Cingalese with diverting combs in their hair and the jolly city of Colombo, and a nice damp soothing equable temperature all the year round. Now India is very many things, but it is not merry, neither pretty, neither pleasant, neither controlled, innocuous nor safe; there are no Cingalese and the temperature is not equable. There is a *joie de vivre* and a harmlessness about Ceylon which seem ring-fenced by its coasts. Now this is the more strange because the distance between Ceylon and India is so slight; the shortest of voyages from Colombo—twelve hours will do it—will land you at Tuticorin. Now Tuticorin is in the District of Tinnevelly, and next door is the District of Ramnad, and of all the damnable places——

And in the second place the Civilian desires to say that he thinks it would be better not to go to Ceylon *after* you have been in India either. It is almost certain to irritate you because they seem to be able to do so many things there—and with ease—which cannot be done in India at all. Also it is so small and neat and compact and comprehensible, and establishments are commensurate with duties. And the people are so different. What it is that God and the people there have done to Ceylon, and what it is that God and the people here have failed to do to India, it is beyond the power of the Civilian to tell you; but it is something that makes an enormous and an unsatisfactory and an altogether maddening difference. Agree, then, with the Civilian's conclusion that unless you are going to stop there or are going on to Hakodate or Yucatan or some place with which no odious comparisons can be drawn, then it is on the whole better not to go to Ceylon at all. *Experto credite*—for the Civilian often wishes he hadn't.

The Civilian—dreadful confession—has never set eyes on Bombay; but for people who come to India by way of that city there is nothing more to be said. The Civilian allows that it is quite probably the best way to come, even to Madras, and these people would not be going to Madras, but to some smart and fabulous station of the icy North; there would be a Regiment there and a band and polo, khitmagars and bearers and chaprassies, a cold weather, camels, and a manageable vernacular; in a word, all those things that happen in novels and in the works of Mr. Kipling, but the poor people of Madras never see or hear of from one year's end to another. In that merry place there will be Commissioners and Commanders-in-Chief; and men who shoot pig will be looked upon as a particularly objectionable brand of outsider. Well and good, well and good; passengers are these to the promised land: they enter by the Gate of India and all their roads lie straight and open before them. But they will never know the Edge of India, which might well be the edge of the world; they will never know what it is to be landed through sounding surf and dumped like a sack of paddy on that bare East Coast off which it seems one might so easily slip. No one could possibly feel like slipping off Bombay. To all things there are consolations, and the consolation of coming to India by Ceylon is meeting India on the edge—the raw, rough edge, unshorn, unshaped and vastly unexpected.

A misguided railway company has now built a line which does away with the crossing from Colombo to Tuticorin. Now one leaps lightly from Talaimanaar to Dhanushkodi on a flat ferry-boat called the *Elgin*; but in the days when the Civilian passed that way one was taken out into the middle of the Colombo harbour in a rowboat and there boarded the good ship *Bharata*, and following the excellent precedent of the schooner *Hesperus*, steered for the open sea. Generally, too, one copied the skipper of that celebrated vessel and answered never a word; for that was a passage among passages. The *Bharata* did her best for one by providing the most charming baths of a greyish stone-like stuff which might have diverted the soul of the most miserable, and by carrying a piano amidships; but in spite of all this the elements frequently proved too strong and every one was exceedingly sick. The Civilian, however, for some reason was not sick, but slept well, and rising late beheld in front of him the Edge of India—a flat mud-coloured coast meeting an ochre sea. He is a stout man who can survey the barer parts of the East Coast of India and feel no boding depression, no sinking presentiment or an unpalatable eternity. The Civilian suffered at that hour for the first time from a disease for which he had then no name, but which he afterwards came to know by the name of Infinititis—or briefly Fititis; it is induced by the contemplation of certain slices of India such as the salt-swamps near Madras or the black cotton flats in the middle of Kistna, and is manifested by a vast conviction that all life is an interminable monotonous uniformity, an endless succession of the same things over and over again. Mantalini suffered from it, though he may not have known it. The Civilian stood, then, in the bows of the *Bharata* and looked at the Edge of India and had Fititis. Somewhere very far away there was a mark in the sky that might have been a mountain, but in the foreground there was nothing but two factory chimneys and a number of scattered palms growing, curiously enough, in the middle of the sea. This last was because the good ship *Bharata* came to the end of her tether seven miles out; the rest one did in a launch in a very choppy shallow sea, while immense contemptuous cargo-boats charged and thundered round one. This was the most terrible part of the whole voyage, and several times as one of these monstrous things came driving at him over the crest of a wave the Civilian gave himself up for lost, but on each occasion some demon on board emitted a stream of oaths—or so it sounded—a half-naked devil leapt into the sheets, the sail came round or down and the monster went girning off on another tack. But it is difficult to be happy when you have to sit in full-face view of a double row of hopelessly seasick people and are menaced all the time by demoniac cargo-boats in the charge of raving madmen; and so the Civilian was quite glad when presently they put him ashore at Tuticorin, which has one uniquely terrifying smell and is said—probably quite unjustly—to be the seventh most drunken place in South India.

In this wise did the Civilian set foot on the Edge of India, and as time went on he was privileged to explore it and to see more of it and more. By the Edge of India he would have you understand not merely the actual beach or foreshore, but all that strip of land—and sometimes it is unconscionably broad—that lies between the last hill and the sea. Travelling by those fine trains that run between Calcutta and Madras and those not quite so fine ones that continue from Madras to Ceylon, you have the fortune to bisect this area longitudinally; so that waking in the morning you may regard from one window that noble chain known to geography books—and nothing else—as the Eastern Ghats, and from the other such a stretch of flat as you have rarely seen, carrying you straight into the rising sun. If you were to alight and make your way across these flats you would pass through a scrubby sort of country punctuated by irrigation ditches and great herds of the insane-looking Indian goats, and you would see around you an immense chessboard of fields separated from each other by little raised bunds like the place Alice saw in *Through the Looking-Glass*; these are the "Survey Numbers" of Mr. Ramaswami Naidu, the Tahsildar, and Mr. Venkata Rao, the Revenue Inspector, and these have inscribed them all in maps and registers, with which, pray Heaven, you may never have anything to do. All sorts of stuff would be growing there, all that variety of cultivation over which morning and night the Indian ryot slaves and toils—paddy in all its sorts, nice, cool, wet, bright-green squares; cholam which grows tall enough to hide a man on a horse, and an immense number of different kinds of gram, red, black and green gram, horse gram, Bengal gram, and Heaven knows how many more, varying in appearance from a tall shrub like tea to a stuff resembling parsley. You would see groves of vastly overgrown lettuces six or eight feet high, and these would be gardens of plantains, that is to say, bananas; and you would see plots of varnished cabbages which would be tobacco. You would come here and there to a village of huts with the blue morning smoke hanging round it like a mist and the local ladies all busy describing intricate designs with ash upon their doorsteps. And having penetrated all this, there would come—quite suddenly—the sea. There might be a range of low sand-dunes or a patch of bare ground covered with a sort of prickly weed or there might not; quite probably, right at the back of someone's paddy-field, there would be the sea rolling in at your feet and the whole Bay of Bengal in front of you extraordinarily big and empty. And if you did not then jump back with the feeling that you had suddenly fallen off a continent, it would be little credit to your imagination.

At home you come to the sea by cliffs or downs or long beaches of sand, and when you come to it you see ships; on the Edge of India, as has been said, you come to it in the middle of someone's field, and when you look there are no ships. You may sit a whole day—and many whole days—watching the sea pouring in endlessly and the little tomato-coloured crabs running this way and that, and a certain indefatigable and rather brainless kind of worm that always bores a hole just below the mark of the last wave and has all its labours spoiled by the next; and now will come the Ancient Mariner's albatross or something like it, and now a flight of duck; and the day will pass and the east redden again—there is always a fine sunset in the east in India—but never a sail will you see. If there be a port anywhere near—or one of those sad townships that used to be ports before they silted up—it is just possible that a coasting cargo-boat, a big, roughly-made affair carrying a single enormous sail, may reward you by an appearance, or that towards evening the natives of the nearest fishing village—which do not approach an you have a sense of smell—may launch with strange sounds a primitive kind of craft, three or four planks tied together with string and ornamented with a design like the Dancing Men cipher of

Sherlock Holmes: on this contrivance they will by some magic put out to sea carrying their nets, and to show that there is no deception and that the whole thing is pukka magic they will dance thereupon like dervishes till your senses reel. But the trail of the liner or the smoke of even the tramp steamer will never come your way. Some told the Civilian that this was because right out to the limit of his vision there was no depth; but the Civilian prefers the other version—that the sea is an Enchanted Sea and that no ship from the outer world can come therein. The enchantment was laid upon it by a magician from Haiderabad—all magicians come from Haiderabad—a very long time ago; and he said that the Dutch and the French and the English might come and take away their ports from the Indians, but they would get no good of them. He was a sound magician and they never did, and thus it is that you see no ships from the Edge of India.

"There you go," said the Superior at this stage, "maundering about magicians and missing the opportunity to record some interesting ethnological remarks about the fisher-castes. You should say, for instance, how the Mahapyas in Tanjore at their weddings make the bride kiss the groom's right big toe, whereas among the Sallas of Godavari it is done the other way round. That's really worth noticing." The Civilian thinks that you will not mind very much one way or the other, but the Superior wanted him to tell you, so there it is, and an interesting fact too. The difference between a Mahapya of Tanjore and a Salla of Godavari—these are not the names the Superior said, but something near enough—the Civilian could not tell you; but he *will* tell you what astonishingly fine figures most of these men who live on the Edge of India possess. They are as straight as a die and big strapping fellows of whom Müller or Sandow might well be proud, and the muscles that come from hauling nets and pushing heavy boats through the surf are simply tremendous. And the Civilian wonders why in these days of universal recruiting no one has made them into a Regiment. He fancies that they like the Edge of India too well to leave it,—it and their little villages set among the coco-nut trees; and the easy life, an hour or two's tossing in the morning with the nets and then blissful peace. Indeed at one place to which the Civilian came in his wanderings they did not even as much as this, for there was a calm and sheltered backwater, and in this they spent the whole day up to their necks dragging little nets to and fro. The Civilian thinks that there might be many lives worse than this—the warm sand and the blue and musical sea and the gods almost putting the food in one's mouth.

From a scenic point of view the Civilian is forced to admit that in most places the Edge of India does not excel; it is flat and undistinguished and tends to induce Fititis. In the course of his explorations, which were long and thorough, he did find one solitary and gemlike bay, wedged in between two small headlands wherein the waves burst and roared and swung from wall to wall even as they did in the nobler seas of home. That bay might have been anywhere, Cornwall or the Banffshire coast or Stonehaven or the Mull of Cantyre, and if you doubt this he will show you pictures of it with the waves rolling and leaping all white and cream on the rocks and the shelving beach, so that you can almost hear the roar and drag of the undertow; but there is only one of it to his knowledge, and the Edge of India is a long, long country. The Civilian has come to the conclusion that it was meant so to be, and indeed it does not make any sort of success of it when it sets out to be otherwise. There is a bit of it known to the Civilian where every now and then hills come down to the very beach, but instead of ending in cliffs and caves and breakers as they ought, they face up half-heartedly and end by producing a dismal effect more like a spoilbank or a quarry rubbish heap than anything else. They carry no green upon themselves and the sea gives them no help in the way of seaweed, and altogether they are a failure; so that even at the risk of an attack of Fititis the other thing is less disappointing.

Once, though, at a place called Waltair, the Civilian came upon a hill standing out into the sea that ended in real cliffs, a pedestal of fine grey cliffs with the sea beating up under them; and he took heart of grace and thought that at last the Edge of India was going to do something for him. So he pursued his investigations along a pleasant carriage-road, but the place turned suddenly to a nightmare country of red rock—bright red—all ribbed and twisted and torn and gutted with torrents of water in the rains; and the Civilian knew that it was India and that it had tricked him once again, and retired cursing himself for expecting anything else. He was undeterred, however, and went on northwards up the Edge of India, and presently for his reward he came to a very haven of peace called the Chilka Lake, a great backwater locked in by wooded hills and full of charming islands with pleasant names. And there he fell in with some very kind and hospitable people, which, in spite of the books, one does not always do in India. On the shore of this lake there stood the Palace of Rambha, which is really only a biggish bungalow but wherein the rooms are numbered and labelled like the rooms in an hotel; moreover, it contains—or did when the Civilian went there—three Orchestrelles and nine-and-eighty photographic cameras. But we must not get away from the Edge of India as the Civilian found when he wandered a little beyond the end of the Lake and came upon a terrible flat swamp and a salt factory in full blast. Then he knew he had been deceived yet again and gave up the Edge of India as a hopeless case.

Some day some one in a monumental work will write of Salt Factories and of those who dwell therein, but first he will require a lifetime's study and must take upon himself the knowledge of many things better unknown. For the Salt Department, you must understand, is by no means all salt; it is the Salt, Abkari and Customs Department, and Abkari means Drinks and Drugs and stands incidentally for much mixed and intricate roguery. So that the writer of the book would have to learn all about "pans" and "garces" and "standard strengths" and "tolas" and the exact status of a Sub-Assistant-Deputy-Vice-Inspector (Acting) and the correct procedure when you find hundred-rupee notes in your topi; and then perhaps he will give us an answer to many oft-asked questions. Such matters are, however, of little profit, and in any case they are mercifully beyond the scope of these pages. The Civilian never understood them; he always regarded salt factories as pleasant places, a little trying to the eye perhaps with the staring white of the ground and the extraordinary collection of odd poles and masts that protrude mournfully all over them; but withal very soothing to the dignity. For the Salt is nothing if not martial; long rows of peons garbed in khaki leap out of the ground at every turn saluting briskly to words of command, and on the slightest provocation these will seize and loose off long Police carbines—blank or ball, it's nothing to them. Also the minor officials of the Salt are the jolliest fellows—bright and capable and friendly as though they had never a care in the world. But they do keep dying suddenly, and as this does not happen among the Police or the Public Works it must be due of course to the innate depressingness of their Departmental duties. There is a bungalow not a hundred miles from

Madras much frequented by the Salt, and it has three graves in the compound; and there the gruesomely-minded can point you out three separate bullet-marks on the wall and will talk horridly of Stains—stains no paint can ever conquer, no whitewash or chunam obliterate. But these things had better be left to the writer of the monumental work; let us back to the Edge of India and the prawns and the sea-snakes and the genial tomato-coloured crabs.

The Edge of India is cut across at intervals by great rivers of a rather depressing character. The Civilian saw most of them and found them all very much alike—great wastes of sand for most of the year and sweeps of blurred yellow water in the rains. They do not greatly contribute to the scenery and are rather a nuisance than otherwise, inasmuch as they are an insuperable obstacle in the path of roads. Godavari is much the best of them; Kistna is a holy river and has his points, but he is all drained away to irrigate thankless delta Districts, and so there is generally very little of him left. But Godavari is something like a river as they know who have even ridden over him in the train—a great giant of a fellow with rose-coloured banks bearing along islands on his back like so many boats. Further up, the Civilian has been told, he comes through a range of mountains and there he is very magnificent to look upon; and down toward his mouth is to be found an excellent kind of man owning large hollowed-out boats in which you may go for many an exciting sail, tacking along flat on her side so as to make the best use of the wind and the current and the tide setting in from the Bay. For this indulgence Godavari demands an occasional sacrifice in human form, and gets it—though it is said that he will not take from among those bold adventurers who go forth upon his waters. Once upon a time some friends of the Civilian went forth in a boat and the boatman being a shade too clever capsized them into the river, and they would certainly have been drowned—for they could not swim—had not Godavari himself washed them ashore on a plank. But when they arrived home calling loudly for hot baths, behold, the *mali* running with hot water fell and was scalded, and a peon rushing to the scene of his outcry—not to help, of course; peons never help; but simply out of curiosity—was bitten by a snake and died. Thus Godavari had his sacrifice, and on the whole the Civilian cannot be sorry that it was a peon. Be this as it may, the Civilian was always careful to make salaam to his Ganesh—it is mere folly not to have a Ganesh in the house in India—before he set forth, and he would offer up a small prayer of thanksgiving to the God of Mariners when he found himself on shore again. From the Fable of the Godavari and the Snake-bitten Peon, however, we may learn how absurd it is to trifle with the superstitions of India; and the Civilian would beg you to keep this ever in mind. . . . At the Godavari mouth there is a fine breeze blowing and there is a wonderful —and wonderfully hidden—old temple which you may find if you are unusually fortunate; otherwise to go ashore is foolishness, for you will only come to another salt factory.

But in his peregrinations along the Edge of India the Civilian did indeed find one place the name of which wild horses will not drag from him, for he has so far succeeded in keeping it to himself and has a mind to continue in so doing. Here there is a beach of pure white sand—not very big, it is true, but quite big enough—and here one may sit contentedly and allow the warm waves to break over and around one. There are no villages near, and hence no fisher people come; and though the Civilian loves and admires the fisher people, he is constrained to think that this is just as well, for the simple fisher folk, they and their sisters and their cousins and their aunts, have a way of lining up and gazing at Civilians sitting in the surf that he finds disorganizing. Possibly there are snakes, but the Civilian never saw any, and so he set them down as an invention of the Cold Water School, a body of persons so-called from their remarkable capacity for throwing that element upon any single thing one may suggest, and of whom—for they are a great and powerful clan—he will yet have to make some mention. But it is not to be denied that there did arrive at intervals large shoals of dogfish—or what the Civilian took to be dogfish—long-snouted mud-coloured creatures which came up in great form with one wave, lay for a space on the wet sand and went back like torpedoes with the next. The Cold Water School said they were dangerous, but they never lived up to this character and took no notice of the Civilian as he sat in their midst. Nor for that matter did anything else; the crows sat in a row along the last wave-mark, one crow to six feet, snapping up that imbecile kind of worm before alluded to; the crabs ran this way and that; the great brown and white kites sat sentinel-wise on the pieces of driftwood; and an occasional jackal came up over the sand-dunes, regarded the Civilian for a space and said distinctly—or at least looked it—" Well, I'm damned!" Having sat in the sea for hours the Civilian used to return to his tent, and as the night fell darker he would see the fires of shepherds and field-watchers springing up all round him. Presently these too subsided, the watcher in his little perch above the cholam field sang his last sad song, and there was nothing left but the sound of the sea, the jackals and the noisy birds that habit the Indian night.

At this place, too, the Civilian saw tropical butterflies hanging upon Christmas trees. The trees were casuarinas and the butterfly was *Papilio Hector*, but as this should convey little to any decently-minded person it will be further explained that the trees were like a plantation of young Scotch firs and the butterflies were very large with black and scarlet tail coats and bright scarlet bodies. They hung by their legs from the branches of the trees and never seemed to do anything else, and they could be taken off by the hand and put back again. As for the trees themselves, those who live much on the East Coast praise Heaven daily for the casuarina, for wherever it appears it is the saving—and if you happen to be Scotch, the making—of the landscape, and is above all the prime factor in making things look like anywhere on earth but India. And this, by the way, is a strange thing that demands some explanation—the utter and sustained failure of India to appear as it is supposed to be. The Civilian very much wonders what you, his masters, conceive this part of India to be like; because if you happen to be anywhere in the British Isles it is not really so very unlike the place where you are now sitting. This is a great heresy, but it is true; the tropical forest of palms and flowers and gorgeous creepers, the elephants and the brilliant birds, where are they? Lo, there are mangoes and jacks and tamarinds and babuls and sirises which are not unlike any other hardwood trees, and as to flowers the best we can do for you without a gardener is the water-lily, and in birds the kingfishers and the jays which do not sound so exotic somehow as they should. It is a genuine shock when a hoopoe or a hornbill or an oriole or some such creature obtrudes itself. The Civilian could set you down in whole miles of landscape in this very Presidency which you would swear you had seen before somewhere in the West of Europe. Perhaps the North of India looks like itself, for the South certainly does not; but then Mr. Kipling—who should know pretty well—says the North doesn't either, so one is forced to the inevitable conclusion that there is no such thing as Indian scenery. In any case it cannot exist where there are casuarinas. They know how to value the casuarina who have looked with weary eyes upon a row of toddy-palms like so many well-worn shaving-brushes standing on end, clanking their horrid leaves like dry and long-dead bones.

At this place of the Civilian's, then, topes—oh, lamentable and hideous word, but it must be used, and, indeed, a brave man once put it in the title of a novel—of casuarinas came down to the sand-dunes, and at that hour of certain Indian evenings when you are lit by the sun on one side and the moon on the other the Civilian used to stand on a floor of lavender glass—it was really wet sand—and survey a Russian landscape of drifted snow and pine forest; which was the white sand-dunes and the casuarinas. Then he remembered he was in India—and "the India of the picture-books" at that—and went home to dinner feeling that he had had another narrow escape of falling off the Edge.

Upon that Bay into which he would have fallen the days are nearly always blue, and it is a kind warm sea of little waves doing no one any harm. Not so always, however—witness Masulipatam. The admirable volumes prepared by the railway companies of South India describe Masulipatam as "a place of great historical interest," and so no doubt it is, for to begin with it was the port of Haiderabad in the good old days when there were diamonds at Golconda, and thereafter it became a milestone, and one of the first milestones, of the British Raj, and was the scene of one of the most remarkable military exploits ever undertaken. This is all very true; but do not go there, for it is a place given over to devils and peopled by the ghosts of long-dead failures. The Dutch came there and failed, and the French came there and failed, and the British brought their luck there and tried to make it a military station, but it killed them off like sheep and they gave it up; and all these peoples have left some of their dead there to groan and curse and set a blight upon the place until the Last Trump is pleased to let them out of it. Take it from the Civilian, that is a gruesome city. It is a place fey and inhuman altogether; this the Civilian found out when one evening, riding about, he came suddenly into a vast dismal swamp of bare brown earth dotted over with ruinous brick-work graves. At the end of the swamp there was a yellow bridge and behind it rose a clump of what looked like Lombardy poplars. Now the Lombardy poplar is a soul-chilling tree and it has no right whatever to be growing in India. Perhaps you may have heard an efficient rendering of Saint-Saëns' *Danse macabre*; if so, it was a place like that. The Civilian gazed at it and in an instant he was seized with terror and despair, so that he fled the place as hard as he could go and believed ever afterwards in a Personal Devil.

Now this swamp was one of the swamps made by that same blue Bay many, many years ago, when, one of its Rulers being angry with Masulipatam, it sent in such a wave as never man saw before or since. The Civilian can tell you about it because he sought about till he heard the tale from a man who had been there. He was an old man and he told the tale many times, but always in exactly the same way because he could never forget any of it. That was a night; when the lock-gates of the new canal were taken sixteen miles inland, and the houses of the place came down upon their people in the roaring darkness like houses of cards, and thirty thousand men and women were left lying about the face of the land all in their jewels and their best clothes, because, poor devils, they were holding Dipavali, which is the Feast of Lamps. There are many dismal places on the Edge of India, as is natural owing to the "great historical interest"; but, of all that the Civilian saw, Masulipatam was the worst and the least redeemed, the most utterly blasted and damned. It is better to avoid such places, for there is no good to be got by going and looking at them, and Heaven knows what relics, what ghouls and vampires may hang around their awful precincts. "Clive kissed me," says Madras in the *Song of the English*, "wonderful kisses"; but these same kisses have left their mark like a brand and to-day they are not pleasant to see. At home ruins may be kindly and even comforting, for there they are ruins of stone; but in India the ruins are ruins of brick and are very terrible. There is solace to be gained from meditation over a crumbled mediæval keep; not much from meditation over the remains of a brick-built cantonment. There are grim, rain-discoloured racquet courts and band-stands and horrible cemeteries. . . . Let us leave such places alone and remain thankful to whatever gods there be that all kisses do not come to this.

And the villages of the Edge of India, the thriving paddy-growing villages whose past is so long that they have forgotten it and whose future is so insignificant—and so certain—that it is not worth speculation, these are not particularly beautiful either. They were there before the ruins and they will be there, much the same as they are now, after many other things have become ruins in their turn. Half the year, while the rains fall and the streams spout and every tank and irrigation channel is lapping over with brown flood-water, they are set in a bog of mud, and therein their people wander and struggle, dragging their carts and their bullocks hither and thither through the mire, patiently going about their lawful occasions. For the rest of the year there is a sky of brass and a heat-haze that levels down all colours to a greyish-blue and a dancing mirage through which one can scarce distinguish the huddle of red-and-white houses from the toddy-palms and the dark-brown earth of the fields. Penetrate into the village and it will be as all other villages; animals and children wandering and rolling in the streets, house crowding on the top of house, rending odours that assail like blows. Outside on the tank-edge there is an imposing structure of shining white, tricked out nobly with a red lion, a lemon-yellow tiger and a blue god; the mausoleum of some man of wealth, a sowcar or a moneylender as like as not, who screwed the money that went to build it out of the skinny wretches who point it out to you to-day. That is the appearance, the outside, of the village; into its real self, its inner existence, its interests, its politics and its beliefs, it is not you who will enter.

For all reasons, therefore, on the Edge of India it is best to get to the very Edge. Otherwise one is apt to be entangled in deserts which are bad, or deltas which are worse. Best of all it is to sit in the warm waves on the warm sand and look out upon that absolutely empty sweep of sea. Then one may feel that the ancients were perhaps right after all, and that the world is a thing like a plate with a rim to it and the loud-sounding Oceanus going round outside. Upon this rim of the world one sits with one's feet as it were dangling over; and even if one never does fall off there is always the pleasant feeling that some day perhaps one might.

II

HEADQUARTERS

NOT so very long ago the Civilian travelled along in the train with a man who came from Calcutta ; and the Civilian in a weak moment asked this man what Calcutta was like. " Well," said the man, " there are times when it's really hard to believe you aren't back in London. Say a Saturday night in the garden outside the *Piccadilly* "—this may not have been the name he said, but it was something equally homelike—" with the band playing and taxis and trams and motor-buses and motor-lorries and all the rest of it." He went on to speak of restaurants where one dined and listened to good music and theatres where one saw plays performed that were even then running concurrently in London—not exactly superbly rendered, he admitted, but still very tolerable indeed when you could get nothing better.

He drew pictures of great streets and boulevards blazing with light, of careless and happy people going to and fro, of concerts and race-meetings and all manner of Metropolitan things. Finally he invited the Civilian to come and see for himself, and the Civilian is going just as soon as he can get the chance. He would like to see a Headquarters like that, for so far it has not come his way. Madras is old and spacious and noble and exalted, but it is not like that at all. There are no theatres, no, not a single one; and in that city the stranger with a taste above picture-houses cannot in any way amuse himself. The natural result is that the stranger avoids it like the plague, thereby missing some little interest for himself and in no wise assisting Madras. Now loyal citizens in a walled city are a goodly thing to possess; but neither is the stranger within the gates entirely without his uses.

It is a vexed and open question whether Madras is the most charming place in the world or the most utterly wearisome. It is a question which seems to depend, firstly, on how long you have lived in it, and, secondly, what position you have held within its walls. They who have lived there for untold ages, and whose fathers and perchance whose fathers' fathers have sojourned there before them, describe it as a very wonderful place, full of amusements, where there is always something going on. The Civilian's father never saw Madras, and he doubts whether his father's father had ever even heard of it, and he himself has never really lived in it, so he is compelled to take this on trust and believe that it is indeed so. He can only say that it does *not* look it. And there *will* creep into his mind the legend of the Three Grey Sisters whom Perseus met in the Unshapen Land, who had, you remember, one eye and one tooth which they shared amongst them, and who sat on a block of ice and thought they were having no end of a time. . . . And it is also true that most people who have not lived in Madras will tell you that it is perfectly damnable.

Mr. Kipling has insulted Madras not once but many times, but then he only paid occasional visits to it and so did not really give it a fair trial. Going on these lines one would make acquaintances in Madras—if one tried very hard—at the rate of about two a twelvemonth. Moreover, Mr. Kipling did not make some necessary allowances; he did not, in the language of the G.O., "adjust himself to local conditions." Every one who has ever read a G.O.—a Government Order, that is—must know how important it is to do that. A lady in Madras once said to the Civilian when he complained of feeling dull, "Well, anyway we don't get Plain Tales from the Hills written about *us*." This was said at dinner, and, speculating over the port afterwards, the Civilian came to the conclusion that the rejoinder was apt and that this great truth was really due to the Climate. All things in India are due to one of two great causes, Liver or Climate; in Madras, then, it is Climate. If one got a North of India cold weather or a cold weather in any way worthy of the name, one might conceivably rise to a Plain Tale; but then one never does. One remains all the year round in a beautifully enervating atmosphere like a warm bath, not quite so warm at some times as at others, but always enervating; and the subjects upon which one's mind runs are bed, fans and drink. Now to carry one with any decency through a Plain Tale, one requires the light bounding step of youth, the flush of enthusiasm on the cheek, the surge of energy that will not be suppressed. Such things in Madras become absurdities; it would be like going for a brisk walk in one's tub. Mr. Kipling did not allow for this. The climate of Madras runs to getting into the billiard room and taking off one's coat and calling for a succession of long drinks, but it emphatically does not run to Plain Tales from the Hills. There is some consolation in that, too, if one comes to consider.

The Civilian is aware that he is not telling you much about Madras, but if there be a Benighted Presidency, then its Benighted Headquarters should be typical of that same and one must examine the symptoms and weigh these great accusations. The Civilian does not think Madras is Benighted; he thinks it is merely elderly. Mr. Kipling's people, who seemed to be setting up a sort of second Devonshire in the Punjab and shouting about it accordingly, should have remembered that they came on much, much later in the scheme of things. Clive's own self has trod the precincts of Fort St. George; there are papers bearing his handwriting within its keep; the guns of the French frigates have roared and rattled outside in the days before Napoleon was thought of; just a little way inland are Arcot and Jinji and Wandiwash and all the great names of the early days. Good friends of the gay and sparkling North, do you possess by any chance in any of your strongholds the authentic bones of a Saint? Can you show us monuments and tombstones dating from the fifteen hundreds? Can you point and say: "Lo, here stood the first British house in India and hence are sprung the Viceroy in Council and all the British Raj"? Nay, for you are young and fresh; and Arizona, for example, is younger and fresher still, but the Civilian does not know that Arizona is the ideal abiding-place. He will not call Madras Benighted; he will call it Venerable. "But is it not also just a trifle stodgy, just a shade behind the times, just the least thing in all the world—Provincial?" Well, perhaps . . .

Well, anyway, Madras is Headquarters. Here the Secretariat, which is the outward and visible sign of the inward and spiritual Government, has its seat, keeping in upper flats of the ancient and beleaguered hold of Fort St. George. This you must still enter by a drawbridge and the narrow portals of the main guard, so that when you meet Sir Narayanaswami Shastriar driving out in his fifty-horse-power Rolls-Royce one or other of you must give way. Enormous numbers of people inhabit the interior of Fort St. George—Staff Officers and Accountant-Generals and Chaplains and many others; but they are not so important as the Secretariat. All Civilians despise the Secretariat and would not accept employment in it for anything; and many are called but few refuse. . . . Scattered about here and there among the peons and the Secretariat clerks and the City Police you will see the dear fresh Tommies from home; and surveying your own yellowed and leathery visage in the glass will reflect what an extraordinarily red-faced race the

British were meant to be. If you ask a Tommy what he thinks of Fort St. George he will tell you; but the Civilian will not write it down here. . . . There is also in Madras the Board of Revenue inhabiting what was once the Palace of the Nawabs of the Carnatic; and next door is the Senate House which misguided people have been known to mistake for the Taj Mahal, and which in spite of its name is mostly used for examinations and concerts. Moreover, there is the High Court standing on an island in the middle of trams and railway trains, and the Great Crime of the cruiser *Emden* is that it just missed one of the High Court's truly wonderful towers. Now if it were not for a High Court, how could there be vakils; and if there were not vakils, how could there be Local Self-Government for India? The Civilian fears that he has now exhausted the places of interest in Madras, for which he begs to apologize. There was once upon a time a German Staff Officer who made a tour in India—where everybody was much too nice to him—and wrote a book thereon; and in this book he added to the gaiety of nations by seeing (among other things) "camels, elephants and mules" in the "narrow, dirty streets of Madras." The book is called *A German Staff Officer in India,* and is published fairly for all to read. If only the Civilian could see things like these, how much more diverting these memoirs would be; but the truth forces him to declare that he never saw a mule in Madras, that there are no elephants on view within some hundreds of miles, and never a camel in the Presidency. The only things that thrive in the streets of Madras—which are particularly broad and clean—are motor cycles, Ford cars and a pair of huge black bull buffaloes belonging to somebody who makes soda-water. This by the way, just to show that the path of such a writer as the Civilian is strewn with temptations and that not all are so strong to withstand them as he.

But Madras has its points, and they are points worth having. For one thing it must be cheap to live in as compared with other headquarters; you do not have to dress terrifically, for example, and there are only five Clubs to which it is necessary to belong. You scarcely ever—so far as the Civilian could see—go out in the evenings, and that must be the greatest saving. You can only back horses at rare intervals; you cannot by any means buy a stall or a supper. And besides these economical advantages, remember that Madras is on the Edge of India and that the blue Bay rolls in at its feet—though the celebrated surf, which gave such magnificent opportunities to the young ladies of the Georges, who used to land there from their packets, and to the cornets and ensigns who stood by to help, is rather disappointing. There is a princely esplanade called the Marina, where of an evening one may ride along a nice safe tanned track and see all the great and good parading before one—names which resound from one end of the Civil List to the other. That is in the season; it is perhaps more interesting to go there in the off-season when you may see quite different people, not less lordly. There will be the Eurasian ladies of San Thome and the Indian gentlemen of Triplicane; and if one knew the minds of all these people one would be a wise man. You will see there also the middle-class youth of India attired in what is apparently going to be his modern dress—a *dhoti*, that is to say a cloth, a tweed jacket of sporting cut, with buttons on the pockets and a distinct "yoke" at the back—the sort of thing no one but a professional golfer would venture at home—long wispy black hair, and on top of all a most distressing little round pork-pie hat. These are clerks or students, and you will see them wandering in rows along the Marina with their arms round one another. They are indeed a strange sight—so strange that the veriest coolie in a decent turban and loincloth is a relief to the eye—but if you are really in search of curiosities you must turn off the Marina and go to the Aquarium which contains fish so extraordinary that the Civilian thinks they must have been manufactured on the premises and never come out of any earthly sea at all. At the unfashionable end of the Marina you will see the Cathedral of San Thome, which is very old and which, considering the materials with which its architects had to work, is really a very noble piece of building. If you do not think so, you may go away inland and see what has been done with similar materials at the Cathedral of St. George, and perhaps you will like that better. The Civilian doesn't.

In Madras, too, the Civilian discovered a great river called the Adyar, on the banks of which stands a Club that looks exactly like a piece of the old

White City of Shepherd's Bush. Perhaps it is. On the Adyar you may for a consideration row in boats. The Civilian cannot row, and frequently incommoded his fellow athletes, but he liked the Adyar. It is chiefly notable for kingfishers and sunsets; there are three different kinds of kingfisher and a different sunset every night. The kingfishers sit upon a telegraph wire which crosses the river and make suicidal plunges at intervals; two sorts of them—a large and a small—are red and blue just like our own at home, and the third and most delightful is black and white. The sunsets on the Adyar are the most wonderful things, for they always come on after the sun is out of sight. He goes down away up the river behind a bank of cloud and everything becomes chilly and dull; the false sunset in the East dies out and there falls a tremendous silence. You are to wait a quarter of an hour or so and then you must say, "There will be no sunset to-night." This breaks the spell and suddenly you feel the faintest of breezes at your cheek and a wave of orange light leaps up from all sides at once, glowing and swelling and deepening into purest rose. It will last perhaps a quarter of an hour, and for that quarter of an hour you may drift in an enchanted world of colours—the banks and the water and the kingfishers and even your own dull and prosaic self all charmed into a new and rose-coloured existence. At the end of this time the spell will flit as suddenly as it came and the world will settle down to a quiet silver grey in the hope of a moon to come. Now there are sunsets and sunsets, but this sort of thing does not happen except on the Adyar. Sunrise in India is good almost everywhere, but for these reasons the Civilian thinks you must go to the Adyar to see the sun setting. And he will pray for you that you be never, as he was once, cooped up in a boat in an Adyar sunset with the type of person—and they are many—who says, "Oh yes, it would be all right if it wasn't India": for of all conceivable Asses this is indeed the most trying, and the temptation under such circumstances to upset the boat and hold his accursed head under the good suffocating water until he drown is wellnigh irresistible. Wherefore the Civilian will pray that this at least you may be spared.

The Civilian thought he had told you of all the places of interest in Madras, but he was forgetting the Victoria Institute. The Victoria Institute is somewhere in Egmore and you may have some difficulty in finding it, but once found you will be rewarded. In it, in a great and beautiful hall, you will find laid out very nicely specimens of the native work of South India. You will see there *saris* and cloths of spun silk and gold coloured like a hundred rainbows and yet all blending to accord; you will see the carved tables and the fascinating little brass and silver beasts that come from holy Madura; you will see the curious copper-and-silver work of Tanjore; and the wonderful brass fish of Ganjam that wriggle about like live things in your hand. You will see every kind and variety of silver work the heart of man could desire—the genuine Indian *swami* ornamentation which is totally different from anything of China and Japan and in its way more fascinating. They will show you mats from Palghat and carpets from Vellore and lace—of all things—which is made in a missionary school at Dummagudem far away up the Godavari. You will see painted curtains and hangings from Masulipatam—weird of design and workmanship these, as becomes anything emanating from that city of devils; and all kinds of lacquer work; and all the many inventions of ivory and tortoiseshell that come from Vizag. Also there will be the little wooden toy people made at Kondapalle—which is in Kistna, and almost the only good thing to be said for Kistna too—and these must be as good toys as ever were made anywhere in the world. All these will you see; and the Civilian predicts that you will come away with an enlarged mind and a diminished purse; for he warns you that you may buy all these things and that the results of a visit are likely to be, in the financial sense at least, disastrous.

And then there is the Madras Club. The Civilian feels that he ought to say something about the Madras Club, but he is not quite sure what it is he should say. Madras being the Headquarters of Headquarters, the Madras Club is naturally the Ace of Clubs. It is said to be the best Club in India, and the Civilian can well believe that it is; you can lose yourself in it three or four times running, and parts of it are still believed by some to be unexplored. The Civilian thinks it is the only Club in the Presidency which is a convenience and not an institution or a duty; and that is only because it is so large that nobody knows or cares whether you are there or not. You at home with your comfortable house of retiral or rest in Pall Mall or St. James's, you cannot realize the Indian Club and what it means. *You* go to the Club now and then when the mood seizes you, when you want a game or some tea or a drink, and you would not dream—nor would any of the members expect you to dream—of going when you did not feel inclined; but in India the fever-ridden patient or the mother with an infant child must rise and take themselves to the Club not one night or two nights or three nights but every night. It is *mamul*, it is kismet, it is the Law of the Medes and Persians. You may rob, murder, bear false witness and take the name of the Lord thy God in vain and all with impunity; but stay you away from the Club, whether because you are feeling ill or tired or have something better to do, or for any conceivable reason on earth, and see what will happen to you. This is in the Mofussil whither the Civilian will presently go; and what Mofussil is he will explain all in good time. The Madras Club is not like this; it does not care whether you come to it once a day or once a year, and, moreover, there is a restfulness about it, a great and St. Jamesian peace that there is not in other clubs. And here a perfectly terrible thought has struck the Civilian. You will remember what he said about the Madras Climate and Plain Tales from the Hills; well, it is a fact that to this day ladies are not admitted to the Madras Club, and if they enter its precincts at all they must sit in their motors or eke in a little pavilion of their own. Can it be—— ? The Civilian will go no further than to say that he hopes not; for he thinks that when gentlemen cease to take an interest in ladies and ladies in gentlemen it is a pretty poor look-out all round. That would be Benighted indeed. Only it is so easy to be sure about things—and so difficult.

It is in Headquarters of any sort that you get the contrasts, the extraordinary parallels and contradictions of which India is so prolific; and as Madras is the Headquarters of Headquarters, so the contrasts are there the more violent. You turn from the main road into a side street and in an instant you are in a village of coolies; in the highway you left they were selling European clothes, jewellery and motor-cars; here they chaffer for ghi and dhal, haggle over the rice and chillies and cardamoms and gingelly and turmeric that the bitter land has been grudgingly giving up since first there were men to sell and men to buy. As you play your set of tennis at the Club or row upon the river, you hear at no great distance the funeral or wedding drums, the maddening Indian music of pipe and horn and tom-tom that has echoed there through all the years; as you drive to office down the smooth municipal road with its blue and white signposts and its wire receptacles for waste paper, you see the little domed temple prolific in imagery that has known no change; the Deputy Collector calls upon you with the latest English novel in his hands and upon his face daubs of coloured paste made from materials that cannot alter. The tram-car roars and clatters through just such a bazaar as Bernier may have come on in his travels; the Mail train is boarded by people in the costumes of the eternal ages. At the mouth of that same Adyar of which we have spoken there are two little fishing villages, and the inhabitants of these have erected on the dunes above the tide a row of rough clay horsemen gazing seawards. Possibly they represent the spirits of the departed, possibly they are in themselves gods; but what matters is that behind them, crumbling and half hidden by the sand, is an older row, and behind these, buried almost and forgotten altogether, are others and yet others. Each horse has a little cup fashioned in his breast or his rider holds one in his hand; and in these you may find a few grains of rice, a dab of red or yellow pigment—simple offerings made in the hope of Heaven knows what. Outside in the made and metalled road stands Sir Narayanaswami Shastriar's Rolls-Royce; and within twenty yards of it this savagely ill-made group of horsemen fronting the eternal sea.

Now the moral of all this is clear and it hardly needs to be written or read. It is we who are out of place, we who are the irreconcilable element, we who make these fearsome contrasts and contradictions—we and our shops and our tennis and our rowing-boats and our traps and our English novels. They are all as much out of place, as much part of another picture, as Sir Narayanaswami Shastriar's motor among the fisherfolk and their equestrian dead. If we had never come to India Sir Narayanaswami might not have owned a motor and the clerks and students on the Marina might not have gone about indecently clad in sporting jackets and pork-pie caps; but men would still have been selling the ghi and turmeric in the bazaars, still burying and marrying with pandemoniac din, still bending in patient worship before the unresponsive gods of Hind. India is the same as ever, and long after we have vanished it will so continue, just as it was long and long before we ever appeared.

And with that let us get out into the Mofussil, for it is plainly evident that the Climate of Headquarters is not agreeing with us at all.

III

THE MOFUSSIL CAPITALS

THE first question which will obviously occur here is: "What in the name of all odd language is 'mofussil'?" "Mofussil," good sirs, is what you mean at home when you speak of "The Provinces," and "mofussilite" said with a certain intonation conveys in India all the shades of meaning for which you resort to the word "Provincial." The Mofussil is a vast stretch of country peopled, so far as Europeans go, by all manner of persons commonly supposed to be of more or less primitive habits; a congeries of Circles and Ranges and Divisions inhabited by bog-trotting jungle-wallahs attired in twill or khaki and subsisting on tinned foods and whisky: in a word, the whole of the Madras Presidency except the city of Madras. It is a nice question whether Ootacamund—a hill station of the Nilgiris, of which more anon—is Mofussil while the Government resides there or not; but to answer this you would require a man who could say the Civil List off by heart and could tell you off-hand whether a Sub-Collector Second Grade who had divorced his wife came one hundred and seventieth in the Order of Precedence or one hundred and seventy-first. There are such men, but the Civilian does not like them and neither would you.

You at home are fortunate beyond words in that you know nothing of the administrative scheme of your Indian Empire and need care less. You must know, then, that the Madras Mofussil is divided into enormous tracts of land called Districts, and that each of these Districts has a headquarters station. Competent men have been known to say that if Districts had no headquarters stations they would be rather decent places, but so far no one has devised a satisfactory substitute. In many cases, indeed, headquarters have been established in the most dismal, fruitless and God-forsaken spot in the district, but even this cannot now be mended, for once you have made a place a headquarters station it is the devil and all of a business to change it. So there they are and there they will probably remain until some genius invents a method by which all India can be administered by a man sitting in the Hills at Simla and pressing different coloured buttons. Those who have studied the subject say that this is sure to come; and it will be a great day for all of us when it does.

In the fabulous North, gay with uniforms and resounding with wit and epigram, they appear to go in for headquarters stations boasting a hundred and fifty or two hundred Europeans; there they have bands and polo and even dances. But in those places known to the Civilian, if one mustered forty souls all told without being too particular, one could call oneself a very tolerable station indeed.

One *might* get an occasional game of hockey with the Reserve Police, or there *might* be some sportsman who owned a bobbery pack wherewith to hunt the wily jackal, or there *might* be a patch of desert strewn with building refuse where some heart-broken enthusiast had essayed to lay out a golf course, but normally there would only be tennis and bridge and —though not by any means always—billiards. No one can play billiards in the Mofussil, and no one cares whether they can or not; but it makes a good excuse to get away from the ladies. This is reprehensible but true; and as we said before, it is doubtless due to the Climate. And as for wit and epigram, we are dependent on the speeches of the Oldest Inhabitant at the Farewell Dinners to speed the Parting Resident, and on the efforts of the Parting Resident himself who tells us how he has loved us all, endeavouring the while not to thank God too obviously for his transfer. Odd little collections of incongruous people, too small to be a little town, too big to be an overgrown family—these, good my masters, are the cities and capitals of such as help you to secure your Indian dividends.

For some reason it is always in headquarters that people quarrel, and similarly for some reason people always quarrel in headquarters. You never heard of any two persons or sets of persons who quarrelled when they met casually in camp. This, the cynics do maintain, is because in camp one side is usually better stocked or is drawing a bigger Travelling Allowance and so can patronize the other, and the kindness of people in India towards those whom they can justly patronize is indeed a heavenly thing. But whether the cynics be right or wrong, it is all different at headquarters. Uncharitable beings have been known to lay this at the door of the non-camping sex —along with many lesser matters such as the unrest in India and the vagaries of exchange; this the Civilian must deny with cursing because he has a horrid temptation to agree. It is all really the fault of Major Vansuythen. Major Vansuythen, you will remember, was a minor character of Mr. Kipling's who enunciated the axiom, "In a little station we must all be friendly." What the gallant Major should have said of course was, "In a little station we must all put up with a lot," but unfortunately that is not what he did say nor what many others have said after him. Headquarters stations are full of Major Vansuythens, all pathetically well-intentioned, and if in the nether regions good intentions are employed as paving-blocks they are certainly often convertible into headstones in India. In a big station conceivably the Vansuythen ideal might become possible, but in a little station where there are perhaps fifteen souls no two of whom are remotely alike in age, profession, interests or antecedents the thing is out of the question. It is not quite easy to be friends when you know so much about one another as you must in a little station and are yet so completely out of sympathy and understanding. Forced intimacies are not the best stepping-stones to friendship, and there is not much point in being friendly if you are not going to be friends. The Civilian will therefore give it forth that in a little station you cannot possibly all be friendly; and if only the majority would rise and knock the local Vansuythen on the head and say boldly, "Let us agree to dislike each other intensely, and persistently blackguard our neighbours behind their various backs to any one who will listen; let us lie about them freely and abundantly where the facts are wanting; let us impute to them constantly the worst motives as they do unto us; but let us at the same time devote our energies to preserving appearances and getting on together until such time as a merciful Providence sees fit to remove one or other of us to a different sphere of duty"—then there would be no quarrels at all. But the Civilian is becoming bitter; and in any case this cannot interest you: you will never have to live in a headquarters station and so you will lose many valuable opportunities of studying human nature.

Why do people quarrel at headquarters? Well, there are reasons. In headquarters even more than elsewhere will you suffer from the curse of Adam; you must work; you must work hard. If you have betaken yourself into a suitably remote camp there is a chance that the *tappal*—i.e. the post—may not reach you; in any case you will not find the zealous subordinate so hot upon your heels. But in headquarters the clerk is at your elbow just as long and as often as you will allow him—laying piles of papers on your table, inexorably leading before your attention arrears you were doing your best to forget. The Indian clerk if allowed would work twenty-four hours in the day and then grumble because there was not a twenty-fifth; it does not matter whether there is any work to do or not, he will go on doing it—he loves it. And in headquarters, your work being doubled, you have twice as many obstacles in the way of getting it done. You have two great curses to contend with—the perpetual chit and the perpetual interview. All the time you are striving with your legitimate business, behold some wretched menial salaaming on the threshold with a note. A wants to borrow your saddle, B wants you to ride with him, Mrs. C is demanding the return of the papers you borrowed and you must rise forthwith and look for them; all of them must have some sort of an answer. Chit after chit rolls merrily in upon you; and between the chits invariably some one has come "to pay his respects." He may be the Rajah or he may be the Overseer of Minor Irrigation; he may want something or he may not; he may have something to say or he may have nothing; no matter—in any case etiquette demands that you ask him to enter, that you accept his little gifts, that you seat him in a chair and address him on general topics for a reasonable period of time. He then takes his leave and lo! here is a chit from X wondering—curse him—if you have such a thing as a bicycle pump you could lend him. You have and you must go and get it; you have not, you must scribble on the back of his chit to say so. Meanwhile the Head Clerk stands by your side, hitching from one foot to the other, laboriously explaining something you know off by heart—but don't interrupt him or it will double the business—and there is always "one word more, your honour," while the clock ticks on and the mercury rises. No chance of sleep in the afternoon; on the contrary there will be Court. "Court with its train of liars and its great gift of sleep," said some one in the good old days, but the laws do not allow you to sleep in Court now. There will be a multitude of lies to hear, a plethora of weary rhetoric and wrangling by the pleaders, and an atmosphere like nothing on earth. Meanwhile the accused will stare at you. If only the accused would cease staring and would desist from salaaming every time you catch his eye, magisterial work in India might be endurable. Then on top of all this, hot tea swallowed against time, some form of violent exercise, a stifling evening and the same people over and over again. Is it much wonder that the temper stretches—stretches—gives at last?

Meanwhile your wife has had a merry day. In camp, if the dinner is smoked or the food supply temporarily fails in some detail it is not so much matter inasmuch as it is camp and one makes allowances. But in headquarters things must be kept up, and keeping things up with only native servants to rely on is a strong man's work. And as with you, so with her; the work being doubled, the hindrances are doubled also. Her curse is the curse of petty repairs; there will be a carpenter who will haggle for an hour and then go away to take his meals, returning insistently when the unhappy woman is trying to lie down. There will be a *darzi*—a tailor—who must be watched like a hawk or he will steal all the material and all the thread he can lay his hands on. If you are foolish there will be a gardener; certainly there will be a syce whose very essence is Lies; or the easy morals of the cook will have given way again. Every one of these, remember, and every other servant in the house and every workman who comes to the house and every single soul with whom the poor lady has to deal, is leagued to cheat and plot and lie and steal and deceive by every method the mind of a Fagin can suggest or a life of petty piracies inspire. At intervals there will come a *dhoby*—a washer of clothes, a most cursed fellow—who wishes to take away your garments to wash at his own house in order that he may profitably hire them out for wear in the bazaar and use your best bed-linen as winding-sheets for his clients' corpses; and who, being denied this harmless request, will straightway set to and give every atom of trouble his fertile and experienced brain can devise. If only one could give up houses in India, or be allowed to employ tortures, or crib in an asylum that imbecile type of resident who hands over his entire month's pay to his "boy," believes his cook and his syce, and pays with genial and idiot laughter whatever he is asked! That is the memsahib's day. The Civilian once read a book—it was a criticism of Mr. Kipling of all things—in which the ingenuous writer spoke of Anglo-Indian ladies as "idle women so cunningly served" that they had to fill up their time with mischief—or some such rubbish. Reading this, the Civilian called upon his gods and burst into the laughter of one who is tried too far. "Cunningly served"! "Idle women"! And the day of the English lady in India—or at any rate the ordinary English lady—is, upon his honour, as the Civilian has said, a very fighting with beasts as Paul at Ephesus. For such women there should be a nightly palace of entertainment provided, with music and pleasant spectacles; instead there is the Club. Half an hour's dutiful conversation in a solemn circle of both sexes; then he who can bear it no more says, "What about a game of pills?" There is a stampede of males like the bursting of a dam, and your unhappy lady is left to go over the servant worries of the day and the small scandal of the station—and oh, God! how small that is—for a solid hour or so. It will be unlikely that more than two other women in the station know anything even about dress. It is more than probable that everything will be dominated by some coarse and pushing creature who should never by rights have been there and whom no one troubles to silence because they all know that this sort of person will come and come and come again when they are wearied out and done; also she will talk to Ayahs and so hold many deadly weapons. India is full of such people and they always get into the Club; but you *must* go to the Club though it be peopled by devils incarnate and you fit to drop on your feet. Therefore you cannot bring there always the sweetest of all possible tempers. . . . But as Major Vansuythen said so well: "In a little station we must all be friendly."

The Civilian finds that there seems to be a singular lack of geniality in his remarks about headquarters; so he will qualify what he has said by the observation that there are headquarters and headquarters. If one were set to choose one's headquarters—which mercifully one never is—the first consideration which should guide one would be climate, for climate is a great point always and is not liable to change. Secondly, one would have to consider what particular set of one's fellows chanced to be there at the moment, and this is almost more important; there are people in India—the Civilian will be committed to no sexes—who would wreck the Garden of the Hesperides, and similarly there are people who would help one through the climate of Hades itself. Headquarters are liable to vary in the most astonishing degree according to the people who live in them; the Civilian came upon a place once which the gods of Hind never meant for a headquarters at all, but had dowered with every sort of natural beauty and advantage—riding-ground, playing fields, water wherein to boat and bathe—a place designed for mirth and idleness and easy pleasure; but it was peopled entirely by Strong Silent Englishmen who were writing reports on Drainage or Land Demarcation and who did nothing whatever beside. And another he can remember set in a horrid plain of sand and stones where there were gathered together men of merry heart and keen invention and ladies who were ready to face the plains and whose dresses were not made by *darzis*. And yet again like a nightmare he can remember a headquarters which was in every way bad, where the eye was sickened by its surroundings, where dowdy people bickered everlastingly over imbecile trifles, where no one played games, no one dressed for dinner, no one in a word did anything. Fair masters, if you should ever come to visit your Indian possessions and an ill fortune should blow you to this place, the Civilian would have you remember that it is a bad specimen and that there are not many like it. Otherwise you would begin to sympathize with the Unrest in India.

You will know a headquarters station quite easily when you come to it. In the first place you will be struck by the enormous numbers of Police you will see; some in khaki with green caps and some in white with red caps; there is believed to be some distinction between these two kinds, but the Civilian never found out what it was. You will see these Police everywhere, marching about in bodies on open spaces of ground, carrying papers, regulating traffic and sleeping in the ditch. Sometimes you will see a man walking along carrying a Police uniform and a carbine with another man in a garb approximating to that of Adam strolling behind; the second of these is the Police officer, the first is a prisoner being taken into custody. The Police are very musical fellows: they always have a band, and sometimes they have a good band. Their favourite tune is the "Stars and Stripes," a melody designed by Mr. Sousa for heavy brasses and rendered therefore by the Indian Police exclusively on fifes and drums. In the Madras Presidency, however, one lives to be thankful for even this—a very nautch becomes in time palatable. And there is one man in the Indian Police who has, if he cares to claim it, an excellent salary waiting for him on the concert platform; for once the Civilian at dead of night came to a village and a Police Station therein, and inside the Police Station was a policeman singing like Caruso—which is not a common quality in Indian voices. It is just possible that all policemen sing like that in remote villages, but they do not do it in headquarters.

Presently, guided by the Police, you will see a vast building, snow-white with a spotless terra-cotta roof. This is the second sign of the headquarters, for this is the *cacheri*, the head offices of the District. It stands in a large compound, and in the compound is a banyan-tree, and under the banyan-tree are various animated groups scantily clad; these are simple villagers concocting cases for the Sub-Magistrate's court. Here and there, aloof and in deep meditation, pace figures in superior white cloths and black alpaca coats; these are vakils—pleaders, barristers: presently they will have the handling of these cases. *Jatkas*—the little two-wheeled mat-roofed pony-carts of the South Indian city—stand about in the shady places, the lean horses sleeping between the shafts, the lean drivers on the top of them; speculative pi-dogs prowl to and fro warily. In a corner a man sells bright golden stringy-looking sweetmeats, betel-leaf and plantains, and down at the gate a blind man sits howling drearily. Things are exactly as they must have been outside the High Court of

Asoka or Chandragupta or Pulikesin II or any other sufficiently antiquated monarch. Inside, the place is like a puzzle-box: there are so many offices opening out of one another that the brain reels in contemplation. Mainly, of course, it is the Collector's office, which is the hold of a most magnificent—and very influential—person called the Huzur Sheristadar; but away down on the left a steady thudding and pounding marks the abode of the hand-press which turns out the *District Gazette.* To the right is the Treasury in control of the T.D.C. with its double-locked iron door and a bedraggled Police Guard snoring in the guard-room; at intervals one of these rises from his slumbers and rising smites with fearful violence a hanging gong, thus giving to the station the one and only correct time of day. There is a similar gong at the Taluk Office, and in 1835 it was prophesied that on the hour that these two should agree and strike together the world should come to an end; so far, however, we have never been within a quarter of an hour of destruction. What does time matter in India? You will see how much it matters if you penetrate into the interior of this same office, for there you will behold the mainstay of Indian administration—the faithful clerk, sitting on a high stool with his legs locked round and round it, his turban cast aside for coolness and freedom—writing, writing, writing. In the next world there will be a separate department for virtuous native clerks, where there will be set up vast ledgers a mile square and columns of figures for totalling a league in height and one million million registers to be posted and maintained —otherwise they will not be happy. If you do not believe me, enter this office, good sir, and try to persuade one of them to take a holiday; he would not understand what you meant. Government gives him so many days of holiday in the year, but he goes to the office just the same; the only relaxation he ever allows himself is a day crammed full of uncomfortable religious observances. He cannot be induced to look upon life lightly, he will respond to your jests with absolute gravity tinged with a streak of pain. In the evening some of his fellows will play at Badminton in the little court that has been made for them in the compound, striking the ball back and forwards dismally and without mirth; thereafter they will troop off to their homes in the bazaar with their arms round each other's necks. Perhaps when they get there they will become interesting, but the Civilian does not know enough to tell you what they will do then.

There is still one more sign of the headquarters and this time an unfailing one. The Police might be there because of a riot and the office might be the headquarters of a Taluk or Division, but when you come to the Travellers' Bungalow you can have no further doubts. Travellers' Bungalows in India are, on the whole, wonderfully clean and comfortable; some of them, indeed, are luxurious, and a few stand in situations which a prince's palace might well envy; but all headquarters bungalows are terrible. There is a reason for this too. In theory these bungalows are built for the comfort of the traveller—whoever he may be—in reality they exist in order that the Collector and the Divisional Officers and the Executive Engineer and the Forest Officer may not have to carry tents with them when they go forth into their domains; and in the outlying stations where these dignitaries from time to time pursue their ways the bungalows are in a lordly state. But in headquarters these people have all palaces of their own, and thus it is that no one comes to the Travellers' Bungalow except such unhappy wanderers as Recruiting Officers, Inspecting Officials of the Education Department, the rare and occasional bagman, and subordinates of all sorts. These doubtless suffer and do certainly make abusive and caustic remarks in the bungalow book, but as nobody is afraid of them nothing happens. Once when the Civilian was ill he lay in the veranda of a headquarters bungalow—a Travellers' Bungalow—upon a camp bed, when suddenly the matting beneath him exploded and burst into white ants which began to loose off swarms of unhealthy-looking offspring with enormous wings. As the Civilian lay quaking in fear there gathered round a dark bevy of crows, mynas and other objectionable and noisy birds which snapped up these unfortunate aviators right royally. In the midst of this there advanced from the compound two vast armies of black ants which fell upon the white ants with the most determined ferocity. The Civilian's nerve now utterly gave way and he crawled demented from the field and endeavoured to deposit his weary limbs upon the bungalow bed, which instantly collapsed in shapeless ruin and a horde of savage cockroaches rushed tumultuously forth. Thereupon the Civilian wrote rudely in the bungalow book and fled. This incident he now merely recounts in passing; but should you ever find yourself lodged in such a place as that you will know you must be in a headquarters station.

These three, then, are infallible in all headquarters stations; and besides these you will normally meet with a Hospital of sorts (which the Aryan brother shuns like the plague, preferring the herbs and simples, the *mantrams* and magic of the bazaar), a District Court and the offices of the Salt, Police, Forests and Department of Public Works. There will also be a rather depressing church and a still more depressing cemetery not too carefully kept—but these are subjects better left alone. You may count with some certainty on a railway station where the big noisy black locomotives of the south will come with long trains full to bursting with Indian humanity or enormous strings of trucks and vans laden with all manner of extraordinary produce. If you are on the coast there will be a port and a port officer, and you may see a boat coming in once a month or so; and in most cases there will be a Bank and a princely fellow of a banker whose superiors shower upon him all the furnishings and accoutrements that the heart of man could desire and question not at all. Be it always understood, of course, that Government do not care for their employés to starve, but still—— It is possible that there may be a Central Jail, and if so that will be a great resource, for therein you will meet most entertaining and interesting characters. You may watch the wonderful jail carpets being made warp by warp and woof by woof, a forger handling the threads and a commuted murderer droning out the pattern-figures from a card, and you may converse with cultured English-speaking gentlemen who ran seditious papers till they ran them a shade too far; and who, having earned every possible privilege by every possible kind of good conduct, will soon be getting out again to carry on the noble work of emancipation. These will tell you that India was a free country until you came, and you may argue with them if you like, but the Civilian cannot suggest to you any lines of argument because he has sworn an oath to avoid all controversial topics. At all events you should find the jail very enjoyable. On the other hand, your headquarters may be a stronghold of enlightenment and education; this you will know because youths in the street will pull faces and shout curious words as you drive past; and when your wives or daughters go forth of an evening a row of these will walk just behind and will whisper and snigger; this sounds trifling, but in a hot climate and a stuffy evening it can be very irritating. The Civilian would like very much to enlarge on the subject of Education in India, but he daren't. Moreover, this is a terribly controversial topic, almost as bad as missionaries, whom, by the way, you will also find at headquarters. And lastly, if your headquarters has a history you will have a fort with a moat and a great gate and a ravelin and a sally-port and headstone-shaped battlements crowning the walls, and that will be a place wherein you cannot spend too much time, for it can tell you secrets. It may be a trifle depressing and the histories it has got to tell may not be cheerful, but then few histories in India are.

There, then, is your headquarters, a place of broad shady roads scrupulously kept by an aspiring municipality, with all your bungalows in their spreading compounds at one end of it with the church and the Club, and leading away from this the main road taking you down past the Police Lines and the Travellers' Bungalow and the railway station and the minute bungalows of all the lesser European and Eurasian peoples, till you reach at last the roar and clamour, the block and jostle of the bazaar. A toll-gate at one end and a toll-gate at the other, a toddy-shop conveniently near to each; and, between the two, forty or fifty people like yourself and anything from thirty to seventy thousand others, going their own ways aloof and scornful and taking of you, their rulers and administrators, not the slightest notice in the world.

And what is life in this headquarters like? The Civilian has given already one or two indications; he will give now one or two more. In books and in all places where people do the correct and proper thing, he is aware that the whole station rises with the crack of day at 5 a.m. or thereabouts, springs upon its horses and carries on for a twenty-mile ride; he is bound to relate, however, that in all the stations he has seen he has never known this done by a single soul. The Civilian considers that, if one sleeps on the veranda at the shady end, bed need not become unbearably hot till eight at any rate, so that one may rise and have breakfast at a decent hour. He salves his conscience by ordering tea at six and then fresh tea at eight; and he verily believes there are others who do the same. Up till eleven of the day there is no peace in the house and one has to write letters and cheques and orders and so forth while the lady of the house dispenses the rations of the day. Then office till lunch-time and the perpetual chit and the perpetual interview as aforementioned to help you to deal calmly and judiciously with a pile of papers no two of which are concerned with subjects remotely akin. Thereafter, Court. Thereafter, petitioners on all and every subject under the sun. Thereafter, tea and the Club and some sort of exercise till dinner, and after dinner a long chair, a drink or two, possibly a little music—but you will do most of it yourself—an exchange of views upon life in general with Mrs. Civilian who has heard them all before, and then finally and unless there is an earthquake—bed. What say you, my masters: the whirl of gaiety, the rush of entertainment, the glamour of the East? "Is it not a little monotonous?" It is. "Is it not a little tiring?" It is. "Is it not almost, in a way, a waste of life?" It can quite easily be made so. "Is there no way out of it?" There is, and God be praised therefor; unless to Judges or

Secretariats or such poor devils as are chained in the bonds of Prometheus there is always Camp. " Shall we, then, go into camp ? " Sirs, the Civilian is with you.

IV

CAMP IN PARTICULAR

NOT so very long ago the Civilian spent the better part of a month counting money in that strange place the Currency Department, which hives in the semi-subterranean regions of the Fort of St. George aforementioned. The Fort of St. George, you will remember, is in Madras, which is the headquarters of all headquarters, but the place where the Civilian was counting the money was not really in Madras but in some hitherto undiscovered country where things are a blend of highly-coloured magic and the worst aspects of mediæval Europe. It was a mixture of the Arabian Nights and the Spanish Inquisition. The Civilian sat on a chair in a cave while Aladdin's slaves ran ceaselessly past him laden with bags of gold and silver for the Emperor of China ; and when this was over he turned a corner and found himself suddenly in the torture-chamber of Seville.

All around were bolts and bars and grilles ; a man sat on the floor fanning with an odd-looking bellows a pan of blazing coals from which other noiseless spring-footed men snatched pointed red-hot irons. Yet another was concocting a curious mixture the smell of which took one straight back to Albertus Magnus and Nicolas Flamel; this he spread on the zinc and tin linings of boxes which forthwith seethed and bubbled and wilted away as did the palace floor at Iolcos when Medea poured upon it her amiable draught of wine. Strange instruments lay about on all sides, and an evil-looking fellow whose pay-bill might well have been countersigned by Torquemada himself walked to and fro carrying a hideous thing called, they said, a monkey spanner, at the sight of which the Civilian gave himself up for lost. That was a sinister and terrible place.

But upstairs there sat rows on rows of nice clean clerks working tremendously, and over them were the captains of tens and the captains of hundreds. Some of them had been there for thirty years and some of them would be there for thirty more. They told the Civilian that they were always there and had no possible excuse for getting away, and then the Civilian was sorry for them, because they could never go into camp. It would never be theirs to stand on the steps of some lone Travellers' Bungalow and watch all they owned hurled ruthlessly upon bullock-bandies and driven off with desperate clamour into the unknown; it would never be theirs to find themselves with nothing but a horse and a half-empty flask of whisky stranded on the wrong bank of a suddenly flooded river and to know that great feeling of being returned to the elemental condition of lacking food and shelter for the night; never, in the dead of night, would they drive half-asleep in a country cart into some new, mysterious and silent township and wake up in the morning to find how different it all was from what they had imagined. Camp bears certain hardships but many blessings withal; and the greatest is that if you like it at all you are infallibly bound to like your life in India. If you do not like it you had better go home, or grow old quickly and become a Judge.

The Civilian has already felicitated you on your entire ignorance of Indian administration, and he now supposes that you did not realize one had to camp. When first the Civilian wrote home to his admiring relatives about his "camps," they replied alluding to the process as "camping out" and seemed to think he was doing it for amusement or in that emulation of the habits of the American Indian which seems to be the ideal of British manhood. But if the Civilian did not do his camps a kind Government would refuse to encash his pay-bills and would drop unpleasant hints anent his resignation, and so they bestow upon him a delightful thing called Travelling Allowance—which doesn't pay expenses—to induce him to sally forth. At the present moment the Civilian who writes to you is in charge of a portion of India called a Division consisting it may be of two or three thousand square miles; this division has a headquarters, and there the Civilian has a large and comfortable bungalow for which he pays the iniquitous rent of eight pounds a month. But for five months of the year it is laid down that the Civilian shall not see his bungalow, but shall go forth into the highways and byways and inspect and inquire and agitate and enforce and drive till everybody is sick of him. This, be it understood, is the minimum. Counting up and reckoning, the Civilian discovers that he has in actual fact changed the roof that was over his head thirty-eight times in five months, which he thinks is enough for anybody. Frequently, reclining in some shed of mud and thatch or of brick and corrugated iron, or cribbed, cabin'd and confined in a ten-by-ten tent, the Civilian has thought suddenly of that beautiful phrase, " the splendid palace of an Indian proconsul " ; and thereat he has scared the lizards and cockroaches and other aborigines with delighted laughter. But he thinks it as well to record these matters here, because it is a fact that there are people who come out in expectation of nothing but an office table and a leather-covered revolving chair and who would not have come if they had thought it was going to be otherwise ; and the Civilian has within his own experience known the revelation come near to tragedy.

Most of the Civilian's earlier camping in India was done in a houseboat. This was a statement which, when he first made it, staggered his friends and acquaintances at home in no slight degree : camels or elephants or palanquins they would have understood, but they could not quite place houseboats in their scheme of Indian life. Nevertheless the houseboat was a very noble vessel, seventy feet long with slatted shutters down the sides and a little triangular deck with an awning in the bows. There were five rooms in it, a living-room and an office-room and a bathroom and a dressing-room and a kitchen. There was also a cistern for water and a coop for fowls. It is true that the bathroom and the dressing-room did not greatly exceed these last in size, but, still, there they were. There was a flat top on which resided the servants and crew, and there were a mast and sail which could be used to supplement the normal method of locomotion—four coolies down-stream and six coolies up. The whole was in the command of a person called the serang, whose chief qualifications for the post appeared to be a total ignorance of sailing, steering, punting, poling or any of the accepted methods of river navigation; having by the special mercy of Heaven arrived at the close of a stage, he would appear and state that he had fever. Those were wonderful voyages: the serang sat on the flat roof and ate curry; the servants sat at the stern of the boat and trailed their toes in the water; the serang's son, an urchin with a face like a skate, took hold of the tiller and abused the passers-by; and the coolies crawling along the towpath with the line over their shoulders sang endless songs and endeavoured to entangle passing women in the rope. Your simple coolie's heart delights in plain and unadorned themes and his songs consist generally of a three-line solo and a fourth line in which all join in; the tunes to which he sets them are, however, distinctly encouraging and good. "The cotton is ripe; bring the big box to the field," is the sort of thing; but the favourite song, so far as the Civilian could make out, detailed at considerable length a dialogue between an outraged customer and an old woman who kept a toddy-shop and who was accused by this indignant of putting *ganja* in her toddy. However, it was a very good and spirited rouse. There was also a very scandalous song about a ranee, but this the Civilian never fully investigated. This was probably just as well, for your Aryan brother of the lower orders has nothing whatever to learn from Rabelais.

All this, of course, happened in a Delta District, and though Delta Districts suffer from many drawbacks, houseboat travelling is not one of them. It is an immensely soothing thing, and, there being just room for yourself in the boat, it is obviously impossible for your office staff to accompany you. In Delta Districts roads tend to become execrable and cross-country work through the mud and water of paddy-fields is out of the question for a great part of the year ; but those goodly people the Department of Public Works have lavishly intersected the country with canals, and along these you go in your houseboat in great peace. Now and then you come to a sluggish river of sorts, or a thing technically known as a " drain " which is distinguishable from a canal only by officials of the aforesaid Department. Here and there is a lock where a smart Superintendent presents you with the unalterable offering of the Oriental subordinate who has no axe to grind—a couple of small green limes. This is safe enough, but, if you see a dish of plantains or mangoes or a pilau coming, look out, for there is more behind.

At the lock, if you are wise, you will get out and stretch your legs and wander for a little in meditation in the Superintendent's magnificent garden of flowers, while your boat sinks quietly out of sight to the accompaniment of the creak of wheels and the gentle rush of water. Rarely—wonderfully rarely—the even tenor of your way will be rent for an instant by a collision, the serang having for once in a way met a more incompetent idiot than himself; whereupon the servants and crew of your boat will hurl themselves with yells and oaths upon the unfortunate collider, demanding his licence. If it is a passenger boat there will be a panic and your servants will all have new umbrellas the next day; the Civilian always found it convenient on these occasions to be busy with his papers in the back room of the boat. . . . But for the most part you will be drifting gently along interminable vistas of placid water, green banks by your side to shut out the flatness of the surrounding country and pleasant trees to give you shade; you will go broadside on at the rate of about two miles an hour, now smiting the one bank, now the other, the serang asleep, the rope trailing, the current doing with you what it will. There is no sense in hurrying and it is delightfully pretty; you will see monkeys and butterflies in the trees—great towering trees with flowers of gold and flame; and the fascinating hairy buffaloes of India will disport themselves in the water by your side, and so you will go on and on till evening falls and you tie up for the night.

There will be a battle of words here, for it will be the aim of the serang and your servants to tie you up at a wharf with a roaring village close by; this you must circumvent or you will have no sleep and boats of dried fish will creep up in the night and hem you in. There is something about a houseboat which attracts the carriers of dried fish beyond resistance, and the smell of dried fish will wake from stertorous slumber the soundest sleeper that ever was. Tied up, then, in some quiet and open reach and dining on the deck, the traffic of these strange waterways will pass you by—great lumbering tatter-sailed paddy-boats sunk to the gunwale with hundreds of sacks, the pinnace of some inspecting officer whirling dizzily, the *rahadari* boat—the passenger express—dead silent with a double row of sheeted ghosts on her high decks. And then, just as the peace of night is descending, slowly and surely and terribly, the dried-fish boat will come.

Moonlight travelling on the canals is very good—if the canal be broad: otherwise the serang, having rebounded from one bank to the other fifty times in succession, will find a sandbank somewhere—how is a mystery—and jam you on it in triumph. But given a broad canal and the Indian moon there is nothing you may not imagine, no pleasure you may not taste. You will hear in the silence the jackals wailing in the thickets, the distant mutter of the drums that are never silent, and the voice of some herd or wanderer on the bank scaring off snakes and ghosts with long cadences of rambling song. There will be ghosts upon the water—ghost boats that come up and pass you with never a sound, a noiseless figure, pole in hand, gliding along their roof, and there will be countless eyes watching in the dark.

Once when the Civilian was sailing down the biggest canal of all, steering straight on the Southern Cross, he came to a sad and terrifying place, where the canal was blocked by a great mass of silent shipping gathered round a village on the bank wherein hell had been let loose. The roll and thunder of the fearful Indian drums beat up to heaven, and the wailing of mourners, which is only one degree less terrible; lights blazed and leapt about, and there was some kind of illuminated screen painted with awful gods in front of which black figures danced and vanished and came again dancing still. The Civilian, who believes in devils, was going on quickly, when there burst up from behind a row of palms two great towers of flame and smoke, and lo! it was the burning of two very rich men who had died of cholera. The flames blazed up over the huts of the village and the silent shipping, and great clouds of hot aromatic smoke rolled down upon the water, and the moon, which was pale with terror, wrestled with an orange-coloured mist. The roar of the drums rose and hammered at the very gates of Kylas, and the Civilian thinks—though he cannot swear it—that the figures of the gods got down from the screen and ran to and fro among the lights. He went on his way as quickly as he could; and as he went he thought about Local Self-Government and wondered how many of those who stared and shouted in that inferno held school-pass certificates and could have quoted in their sober moments from the peaceful Essays of Elia.

Just to show how one must be ready in camp for all things the Civilian will tell how the next night found him at a wedding. It was a very large wedding and the bridegroom had just bought a motor-bicycle, but for all that he conducted his affairs in accordance with the best traditions of his sires. It was the great night and the Civilian, having expressed a desire to see the procession, found himself—rather to his chagrin, for he was wearing khaki shorts and no collar and had just got out of bed in the middle of the night to see it—the central object of interest, placed upon a chair in the main street so that all might pass before him. And a right fine display it was. The van was held by a body of rather debilitated spearmen, who pushed and howled and made a great ado but disturbed nobody; followed the native music, halting to play before the Civilian. The Civilian does not pretend to understand Indian music, at which he finds himself very stupid, and the more people try to explain to him about *sarmas* and *srutis* and so forth, the more confused he becomes; but he can testify that the Indian pipe, which at a distance of several hundred yards has a charm of its own, becomes at a range of five feet a little trying. But when the "English band" from Cocanada—brass entirely—appeared blending hideously with the retreating Orientals and blasting out a funereal waltz he was not sure that the change was altogether for the better. Followed at last the bridegroom, who had discarded the motor-bicycle in favour of a palanquin covered with imitation pearls costing fifteen pounds a night—no less—to hire, and thereafter the Civilian was sorry that he should ever again see an Indian gentleman in European dress or in ordinary circumstances. He was clad in purple and was chewing betel with an air of such superb and regal insolence that the Civilian sprang to his feet acclaiming at large. Beside him lay the bride—aged seven—sound and peacefully asleep, a feat which the Civilian so greatly admired that he rigorously forbade her to be awakened. (And the virtue of this was seen next morning when the Civilian paid them a visit, for the lady was composed and mistress of herself, but her lord of the purple and the betel-leaf was indeed a sorry wreck.) At the tail-end of all this, and as an anticlimax of the most drastic, came that deplorable form of entertainment, a nautch. There are probably still those who share the views of the Reverend McPherson celebrated in the *Lays of Ind* who "believed that a nautch was a most diabolical sort of debauch." It isn't; it is the most lamentably tedious form of entertainment that ever masqueraded under the guise of pleasure. A number of young but remarkably plain females, cumbered with voluminous petticoats of displeasing hues, executed with the utmost unintelligence a series of graceless and automaton movements; these the Civilian is in a position to tell you represented maidens flying kites, maidens charming snakes and so forth; but he frankly confesses that but for the kind offices of the local Sub-Magistrate he would not have realized this from the performance. Such then is the vaunted nautch—and such is the depravity of the human mind that the Civilian was bitterly disappointed; but Mr. Ramaswami Naidu, a gentleman who knows many secrets, has hinted that there are nautches and nautches, so the Civilian lives in hope. He does not think, however, that the dancing girl is likely to be the future ruin of India, for there is nothing on earth quite so devastatingly moral as unattractively mounted vice.

So much for houseboat camping in the meantime. The Cold Water School—you remember them ?—say that it is unhealthy, that you get no exercise, that the canal water is poisonous and smells intolerably, and that you are always coming upon such highly unpleasant objects as cholera corpses and suicides. As to this one can only say, as one can say with most other dogmas of that depressing body, that either they have been singularly unfortunate in their experiences, or else, as is more likely, that they have never had the gumption to go and experience at all.

After all, Delta Districts are rather an acquired taste ; they are not very easy to like, and even when you have liked them the effect they produce is something hard to convey. They are flatter than anything you could ever imagine, and wetter ; everywhere are little channels running and great creaking groaning well-wheels where the bullocks pull up endless skinfuls of water which goes splashing off into the already submerged fields. They are also infested by black cotton soil which is dreary in appearance at all times and in the rains becomes such mud as might well have inspired John Bunyan with his idea of the Slough of Despond. This and the immense teeming population—there is a village every two miles or so and hamlets in between, and every village and hamlet simply packed and bursting—tend to make for a not inconsiderable depression. The Civilian has spoken already of that unhappy malady he calls Fititis which was first induced upon him by the sight of Tuticorin from the fore-deck of the *Bharata* ; you can get it to an almost intolerable degree in Delta Districts, especially in the cold weather when the crops are off the ground and the fields are one endless flat stretch of black earth. The Civilian could never altogether overcome this, but he did sometimes feel that there was a pleasant peacefulness and security about these seaward flats, and he felt this the more because he was always rather frightened by the Indian hills which are twisted into the shapes of things in torment and frown and glare upon one with faces of sheer and fearsome rock. And so, having gazed rather uneasily upon such places, the Civilian found a certain comfort in the broad flat delta lands, especially when the softening hand of evening had toned down the glare of colours, and the blue smoke gathering round the villages made them look rather pleasant little refuges in the midst of the expanse. One felt that as the night fell upon these dreary latitudes all manner of things might come down with it—devils and ghouls and all the particularly unpleasant Indian ghosts, and then it would be good to be in one of those nice compact villages. The Civilian's first months in India were spent amongst such evenings as these, with the moon rising huge and tawny with the haze and the frogs beginning to roar and bellow all round ; he does not suppose for one instant that he could convey to you what it was like, but he will beg you to believe that there *was* a charm about it and to imagine it for yourselves as best you can.

But in another camp the Civilian found himself right on the top of a solitary mountain three thousand feet high rising straight out of the plain. He was guided up to it partly in the evening and partly in the beginning of the night by an extraordinarily inebriated old man who could scarcely stand and who solemnly warned the Civilian at intervals to go carefully as the road was rough and dark. Finally he got a thorn in his foot and in the attempt to stand on one leg to remove it collapsed utterly. So the Civilian went on without him, and on the top he found a delightful bungalow built by the very noble Department of Forests, and the remains of an old fort built by Heaven knows who. There were also a number of pools and tanks cut out of the rock, and caves and bathing-places; and having eaten and drunk the Civilian sat on the topmost pinnacle of rock in the moonlight and saw all the kingdoms of the earth spread out below. The Civilian abode there many days—the area of the summit being perhaps two hundred yards square—and it is one of the places he means to buy when he retires so that he can live there whenever he likes. On one side one looked out over plains and rivers and temples and villages and cities from which the drums that are never silent in India beat up faintly to one's ears; and on the other there was a maze of green and wooded mountains with remote valleys and patches of cultivated plateaux and lonely jungle pools where anything on earth might come down to drink. India can be most remarkably ugly and very, very often is, but when she has made up her mind that you have been good and that she will give you a treat, she can reward you with both hands overflowing.

And yet again the Civilian penetrated to the region of the Ten Lost Tribes, a place called the Colair Lake in the district of Kistna. It is an interesting place because it is impossible to tell when you arrive at it; you get upon your boat and you sail up the great Salt River or Upputeru and after a time you begin to wander about a country composed of reeds and channels, and at one point of this journeying you really are in the Lake. The Lake is all like this, so that it does not look like a lake at all. You are thrust into the middle of a vast expanse of green rushes out of which here and there rise mirage-like villages on islands of mud; all round you are reeds and shallow water, and you would not know where the channels lay but for the long strings of buffaloes swimming down them from one scrap of mainland to another. The Civilian got himself a pinnace and paddled round and round the Lake for many days, losing himself hopelessly time and again. One set out boldly, and presently the houseboat vanished from sight and one was going down a narrow corridor of ten-foot reeds with the most amazing water-birds splashing and floundering on all sides; followed a huge lagoon of absolutely motionless water, crystal clear, the bottom carpeted with weeds and all the duck in India sunning themselves on the surface. On the other side of this lagoon was a solid wall of reeds; apparently the world ended and there was nothing for it but to go back; but always the aborigine who steered the pinnace knew the one place where there was a road through, and so one would be magically in another dark corridor with the mysterious noises all round one again.

So on for ages—a succession of lagoons and reed-forests, and then suddenly roofs rising out of the water and lo! one had come to an island. Some islands had half a dozen trees, some only one, but the most were as flat as a table and as bare, for the Lake had recently been up in flood and all the crops had been swept away, leaving nothing but the skeletons of cattle and a horrid and poisonous-looking root which the unfortunate inhabitants were grubbing out of the Lake. In some places they ate this only, in others they sallied forth in boats made of hollowed-out palmyra trunks and cast nets for fish, and there were one or two fortunate fellows who possessed antique firearms and could bag an occasional duck. They told the Civilian that they were quite frequently reduced to this state as the level of their lands was only a foot or two above the level of the Lake, and in any case it was a struggle to get a crop in. The Civilian felt inclined to ask them why they attempted to live in such a place at all, but he knew they could not have told him. They did live there and there it was.

Most remarkable of all, on one island there was a fort. It had been a large fort and there was still a circular line of hillocks which had been walls and some curious trees which had been a garden. One of them had a right-angled twist in the middle where it had turned out to avoid a balcony that was no longer there. The only part that really remained was a temple, and the Civilian will record his gratitude to the builders and maintainers thereof, since but for it, standing white and clear on the bluff of the old fort wall, he could not have found his way about the Lake at all. But conceive any one building a fort in the middle of the Colair Lake! It belonged to some family away over on the Haiderabad side, and the Civilian thinks they must have kept it as a quiet and suitable place whither to send those undesired members of the reigning house with whom it was held expedient to make away. The Civilian thought that it must be full of grim and unpleasant stories, and he has no doubt that there were ghosts, but he did not see any. He found it enough to sit on the westward wall of the fort and look out over an endless sea of reeds that went right away into a very red sunset and a row of ghostly hills that were really in another world altogether; with nothing moving anywhere, and not a sound but the pigeons on the temple behind, and far away the tireless drums of the island villagers beating to the glory and propitiation of some cold and thankless god.

In the course of time, however, the Civilian came to a place even more ghostly than this, when he slept a night in the old palace at Kondapalle. Kondapalle is famous nowadays because its residents make comic and diverting toys, but in the old days they went in for sterner pursuits, and it was the base of a great military power. Kondapalle is a modern village with a railway station and all the rest of it, but when you have bought your toys you will strike inland and you will come to a double wall and gates, and when you have passed through these you are in the old Kondapalle and the haunted ground begins. Behind the village there stands up a row of rock hills, very warlike hills and overbearing, and all over these hills there run walls and causeways of black stone and gates and battlements and bastions and watchtowers lost in the jungle. And in a hollow between two peaks of rock at the head of a formidable road, lurking in the pass like a monster of the place, you will come upon all that is left of the old fort and palace of the kings. It fell once by treachery and once to the assault of British arms, and in the plain below—that fair plain over which it still looks out—twenty thousand cavalry and seven hundred elephants have jousted with spearmen and bowmen for kingdoms and treasures. At the gate of the palace there stands to this day the shrine of a holy man, and in the long lonely nights up there with the owls flying about and the jungle creatures rustling and whispering among the ruins he must have some eerie moments; but he is not communicative.

But you may still see and trace the carved pillars of the halls which have known every sort and manner of wickedness, where Hindu and Mohammedan and Hindu again have held successive sway, where treachery and avarice, war, murder, pillage and rape have run their wild course; you may still see the old walled gardens with bathing-pools cut out of the rock where the fair and frail conducted their not altogether blameless intrigues; and in an alcove of one of the old chambers you may at this day obtain an habitation, and there, even if you be gifted with no imagination at all, you may learn at least how ceilings ought to be made. In the morning you may go out and wander along the black stone causeways in the jungle and you will come upon shrines of strange gods and burial-places of nameless people, and wells and ramparts and gates and towers; and somewhere there is a cemetery of British soldiers which holds a Colonel and a drummer-boy and many another stout fellow besides and bears witness that the days of war—and of deadly fever—are none so long departed. And right in the densest of the jungle there is a huge great Hanuman, and the Civilian, finding him, asked him—for Hanuman is a friendly god—what he thought of it all; and Hanuman said that the Old People would some day return and that there would be wars and fighting again—and he should know, for he was once a general and a conqueror himself.

Finally, if your head is sound and your nerve good you shall, for your virtues, ascend to the hill of the highest watchtower, beginning with a scramble among rocks and boulders and ending in flights of cobweb stairs among the clouds with a thousand-foot drop smiling at your elbow. At the summit you will find a thing like a sentry box, and holding on to this lest you fall down on to the plains—as you certainly would if once you slipped—you will see all

India. You will see plain and hill, forest and jungle, field and sea, and the whole course of Holy Kistna for more miles than one can think of. You may see, if you are fortunate, a panther come down to drink at those pools that once received the charming bodies of the Incarnations of Virtue and Delight; you will see the monkeys scamper on those battlements that of yore cast stones and molten lead on the invader, and sport through the halls where grim kings surveyed their prisoners and took counsel in what specially hideous way these should quit this world; and a great eagle will perch himself on the rock beside you and tell you that all is vanity. You will hear the evening rustle and stir of the jungle, the invading jungle that cares for nothing and wanders at will over the workings of all men alike; you will hear the call of peacock and deer proclaiming that theirs is the empire that endures; and you will probably come to the conclusion that this is not a place wherein to spend long periods by oneself. But you will have seen the prospect of a great country and you will have conferred a brief instant with the mocking and scornful devil of the place, and even if you fall off the stairway going down this cannot be taken from you. So find you time as you descend the black precipices of rock to thank such gods as guided you to these ghostly and memorial hills.

Kondapalle was a wicked place in all earnestness, but its wickedness was of old time and so is carried off by a cloud of historical picturesqueness. It was wicked of them to maim and slay and torture, but they would not have been interesting otherwise. But the Civilian will now tell of another place whose wickedness is modern and still continues. It is the seat of an ancient and venerable zamindari, and those who have read Tod on the manners and customs of Rajasthan will realize what that implies. As a zamindari it is quite negligible and its revenue consists mostly of arrears, and indeed it has now gone under the Court of Wards—which is an institution for dealing with wicked zamindars—and so has really ceased to be a proper zamindari altogether; but it is interesting none the less. It claims an enormous stretch of jungly hill country which nobody disputes with it, and it has also a certain area of unkempt plains—mostly mortgaged. It pretends that it was once a great Estate and that its lords were fierce and mighty warriors, but the Civilian does not believe it. For long years back at any rate it had been in the hands of ladies, and the Indian lady, though charming and accomplished, is not a conspicuous success as an administrator. There naturally appeared from all sides the fine Indian gentlemen of fortune, sleek and comely with the Jolly Rodger openly hoisted, scorning nothing from an anna upwards, and whatsoever their grasping hands found to do that doing with all their might. Just where the hill and plain country meet there stands the little town which was the old and established hold of the zamindars with its fort and palace and this is the place the Civilian finds interesting.

It is not by any means a large town, but it is full of tiled houses of ornate design which may or may not represent some portion of the arrears of revenue the estate was never somehow able to collect. Now some of these houses shine resplendent like the sun with paint and chunam and mural decorations, but others are shabby and dismal in the last degree—and these are the houses of the gentlemen of fortune who subsequently gambled and lost. Never were there such glorious gamblers—fighting rams, fighting cocks, cards, horses, there was nothing on which they were not prepared to stake and to stake with an open hand. Some lost and their houses are falling down and their women are dressed in cotton cloths; and some won extensively and their houses are glorious and their daughters wear silk attire, just to show what enterprise on a bold scale can do. You may wander between these houses through street after twisting street and you will see there many memorable faces—faces cunning and bloated and faces merely smooth and impudent and bland. Here and there lying in a shady veranda dictating something to an industrious writer you will come upon a lean man with a shaven head, half unclad, with a cord of threads over his shoulders; and that will be a Vydiki Brahman, a priestly man, who, sitting quietly as you see him, pulls the strings of all manners of wickedness. You will see lurching about the streets the great sleepy bulls of the temple robbing at will, and you will see that no man will lay hand or stick upon them for fear, but little children drive them about at pleasure. And you will pass down the length of an embarrassing street where bright eyes will challenge you and whispers and laughter will follow your footsteps like ghosts; for this is the street of the dancing-girls who are a kingly failing and gather in such places as this in scores. All round you as you walk you will be conscious of a murmurous and secret life not more to be seen openly than these half-guessed forms watching you behind the latticed windows; an immense seethe and whirl of petty intrigue, of the war of sect against sect, of the faction of one scoundrel against the faction of another; you will be in an atmosphere of anonymous petitions—which in old days were stabs in the back—and concocted cases which have taken the place of waylayings with armed men, and forgery which is much the same as ever it was. They are not so exhilarating as the methods of the old days, these, but so much safer; and if an honourable British Government be not intended for the investigation of the petitions of Mr. Akasi Ramayya—that is to say, Mr. Rama in the heavens who is the local equivalent of the Man in the Moon and signs all anonymous petitions—and the consideration of concocted cases and perjured evidence, then what in the name of Heaven is it doing in India? In this town you will find petition writers under every tree and they flourish exceedingly. And if ever you should, after years and years of patient study, get really into the heart of such a place and be able to say who does what and why he does it, you might tell the Civilian, for he would very much like to come in and see.

The Civilian called once on the rather pathetic and bewildered old lady who was all that was left of a family of whom it might be said, in the great words of Billy Bones, that " drink and the devil had done for the rest." She was a nice old lady, quiet and rather tired, and she talked to the Civilian, she on one side of a closed door and he on the other—but he caught her trying to peep at him through the hinges for all that. She lived in what she and her people were pleased to call a fort, but the fort consisted of a mud wall negligible to any sort of attacking force, and the palace of delights inside was a rambling, four-square, unkempt barracks of a place ranged round a courtyard full of the dust of ages. There were a swarm of retainers and menials and general hangers-on, but never a lick of paint for the crumbling walls or a dash of whitewash for the staircases greasy and black with the touch of innumerable hands. The old lady talked mainly of the iniquity of the pittance accorded to her by the Court of Wards, and when the Civilian suggested that if she had managed her estate a little better there need have been no Court of Wards in the matter, she said that the estate had always been very ably managed and there had been no complaints. The Civilian thought of a few hundreds of rack-rented tenants and a few scores of irrigation works mouldering into decay, and he saw that the Ranee's ministers had been worthy of their class; but he said no more, and the Ranee—she was not a real Ranee of course, but they called her so—went on to abuse her sister-in-law who had stolen some of her silver vessels and was now trying to poison her. The Civilian heard this without a tremor, for that was only natural in such a place and quite to be expected; moreover it will never come to anything serious. The sister-in-law will never really poison the Ranee, but she will always go on trying. The Ranee said much more, but the Civilian's attention was hopelessly diverted by the pictures on the walls; these he will not attempt to describe, for unless you have seen a specimen, the bazaar oleographs of the Hindu Trinity and their histories are a type of art the effect of which cannot be put into words. There was one rendering of Vishnu in the Lion Incarnation rending the inside out of a demon and devouring him that for sheer spirit would be hard to beat. In time, however, it got upon his nerves, so he accepted betel and rose-water and came away and left the fort with the undesirables of the place snoring all over it and the lynx-eyed palace officials slipping to and fro and the poor old widow lady sitting in the room of the dreadful pictures quite bemused and most utterly alone.

Not very far from the place of the Ranee the Civilian came into a very holy country, where temples stood every here and there upon hills with flights of stone steps—two or three hundred of them at a time—leading up to them. Now this was not in the south of the Presidency, but in the north and among the Telugu people, and as a result the temples were insignificant to look upon and contained in themselves no beauty whatever. In the south, the holy and Tamil-speaking south, the temples are a sight to see, as any one who has passed by Tanjore and Madura in the train can testify; but then in the south every second place is the residence of some especial god and the greatest of the Hindu trinity has wandered everywhere over it. Also—and this perhaps has most to do with it—there is very much more money. But the Civilian liked the little temples on their hills, and inasmuch as the beautiful temples of the south are set invariably in the midst of a howling city he preferred those of the north. The Civilian had seen the old temple in the fort of Vellore which has stood desecration at the hands of Mohammedan and Englishman in succession and finally—and far most fatally—at the hands of a well-intentioned Department of Public Works, but still contrives to remain a wonder; he had seen that part of it where the horsemen on odd-looking steeds leap at you from the fretted tracery of the pillars; and having seen all this and having some slight knowledge of Madura he cannot say that the Telegus' temples do them credit. If the gods had not helped them out a little with the situations they would be poor indeed. But the places are holiness itself, and on a festival night when all the stairways are lighted with little wicks burning in oil and the tank at the foot flares in red reflection amid the crash and thunder of the drums, there is a fine barbaric splendour that a better building and more costly trappings could hardly attain. And at one temple which he visited they showed him a miracle of local workmanship—a car for Krishna carved in the form of a tree in the branches of which the god could be set surrounded by most wonderful birds and such flowers as are not in any of your gardens. The story it represented was perhaps a trifle discreditable, the god having been caught in the middle of a somewhat characteristic episode in which he had abstracted the clothes of a number of ladies young and old who were bathing. These also appeared in the carving and very spirited they were—one who was boldly ascending the tree being particularly good. The comment of the Civilian's clerk upon this was that these stories were silly but were nice to tell small children. The Civilian wondered.

But the Civilian could go on like this for ever and tell how he went from one camp to another, and some were good and some were bad, and some stood on hills and some in marshes, and some were enjoyable and some were very much the reverse. He would like very well to tell you of every camp he ever had, for when he comes to reckon up soberly there were few indeed that were really unendurable. There *were* one or two, but he will leave them out and so not spoil the picture. And besides and most of all, he has a feeling that if he went on like this much longer he would lose your interest and attention, and that he would be loath indeed to do.

V

CAMP IN GENERAL

IT has been occurring to the Civilian for some time back that in spite of all that he has written you are not going to carry away much of an idea as to what Indian camping is like. He has told of one or two places, but not at all of how he got to them or why he went; he has been putting the particular before the general, which shows what a thoroughly muddle-headed person he is and how totally unfitted for the great administrative positions he is called upon to occupy. He has been giving you too much about camps and not enough about camping. With these thoughts in his mind he gave what he had written to the Superior, who read it and gave it back to him and went out of the room and said nothing. . . . So the Civilian is left to himself to do as he thinks best; which is terrible, for he is a Government Servant and accustomed to referring everything to Section X, Sub-section Z, of one or other of the beautiful Indian Codes, and he hates taking any sort of responsibility upon himself.

Well, then, camping is a question of hills one day and plains another, houseboats in one district, hill-ponies and palanquins in the next, a reasonably good horse generally, and, if you have been very lucky in the place whither you have gone, an elephant. It would not be fair to the German Staff Officer of happy memory to say that people do not use elephants at all in the Madras Presidency, because at the north end there are plenty, as the Civilian can testify, having fallen off one into two feet of mud and water. If you are ever asked to choose your district—which you never will—bear in mind that the elephant is the wisest of beasts and that most beasts are wiser than the wisest man, and go where there are elephants. The elephant districts are always the best. Trains there are, but one does not use them very much because all trains in India are arranged so as to depart from any given station at the most inconvenient of all possible times and yet achieve the miracle of setting you down at your destination at an hour more inconvenient still. Moreover, they are hot and terribly noisy, and at every station men with voices like bookmakers come along selling sweetmeats and plantains and water and milk and cheroots, bellowing outside your window with particular vehemence because they know it will annoy you; moreover, you will nearly always miss your train because of the Indian time-tables, where there are twenty-four hours in the day. It is almost impossible, you will admit, to catch a train which starts at 19.1 or 15.57, yet that is what trains in India are doing every day. It is better to leave them alone.

In the old days, the Civilian has been told, people used to drive a great deal behind spirited horses, which they also rode when so disposed. But the day of the horse in India—or, at least, in that part of India known to the Civilian—is nearly done. This is largely due to one Ford, a maker of motors; and to that soulless but sensible man who discovered that pressure of work and growth of objectionable townships meant that he had to do most of his camping along the main roads, and that it was quicker and more comfortable to drive along these in a motor than to trot along them on the back of a horse. The Civilian likes horses, but he does not like them when they trot; and so at an early stage he took unto himself a cheap motor-car. The Cold Water School instantly said that it would not go, but it defied them and went like anything for four thousand miles when a tyre burst. The Civilian cannot attempt to tell you about Indian motoring, because that would require detailed treatment and a book to itself, but he will ask you to believe that it is different from any motoring you ever did. Bear in mind that the worst road in your county would probably be better than the best road in the Civilian's district, and that some of the more rudimentary of the byways along which he has to coax his car would cause your chauffeur to throw down his tool-bag and strike. When it comes to tackling unbridged rivers three hundred yards across, brown water of doubtful depths and unsuspected potholes in wet weather, heart-breaking banks of soft drift-sand in dry, hitching wheel by wheel over large sugar-loaf rocks in the middle of the road, tackling a gradient of one in three or so straight off a stretch of eight-inch mud, negotiating a right-angled curve on an outward sloping road just broad enough for the car, and crawling with the off wheels half over a gulf past an interminable string of absolutely uncontrollable bullock carts—when it comes to these, motoring is motoring indeed. The Civilian has gone down into the ditch and charged a culvert at twenty miles an hour; he has taken a header through a glass wind-screen—another man was driving that time, though—and he has gone backwards over a khud on a mountain road; and this he tells you not boastfully but in order that he may say that this is nothing to what some men have done. The worst drawback is the bullock-bandies; there lives not on earth another so idiotic and so utterly incapable as your Indian cartman; he controls his animals simply by prodding them from behind or twisting their tails, and as a result he has no means of guiding them whatever; he is nearly always drunk or asleep, and his ideas of the rules of the road are such that you can never tell for a moment what he is going to do next. As a result he leads one to much incoherent blasphemy and to offences under Section 504 of the Indian Penal Code, which is insult likely to cause a breach of the peace, and Section 352 of the same, which is common assault.

You are to picture the Civilian, then, sallying forth into camp by these various methods of locomotion and in all stages of deshabille from pyjamas onwards. Generally one appears in the fine simplicity of a shirt and shorts—and it is more than possible that these last will be of a loud and startling check. The Civilian's modest attire was once described by a candid friend as a "sponge-bag suit and potted-meat stockings"; so you may form some idea of his appearance. Normally, then, it matters little how one is dressed, for there is no one to see but the native, and the native may dress himself in a silk hat, a shooting coat, polo breeches, bare legs and carpet slippers without remark or criticism from any of his kind. But here the Civilian will state that he does not approve of the practice of some gentlemen he knows who receive a spotless Tahsildar or a brilliant landowner or some such person lounging, unshaven for days, in a suit of decayed underwear or faded pyjamas; they would not like it if the Tahsildar or the landowner appeared in that guise before them, and though it is admirable to be untidy and at ease, the Civilian thinks there are limits even in camp. However, let that be. One sallies forth, as the Civilian was saying, in some sort of deshabille with the knowledge that one must cover some sixteen or twenty miles. Somewhere far ahead in the unknown, your peons—those fearsome badged and belted accessories who are now and ever shall be utterly useless to anybody—are alternately sleeping and extorting gifts from the inhabitants of your unhappy destination, the while in the shelter of a grove of mangoes or coco-nut palms the village servants labour to pitch your tents. It is not their work, but your peons will see that they do it. This desired spot you must somehow contrive to reach before night, else will you and your steed be wanderers on the face of a friendless world; and really to enjoy things you must set out persuading yourself that the chances of your ever getting there are remotely small. A river may rise in flood, your horse may run off with you, your motor may be blown away by a cyclone, you may lose the way a hundred times; anything may happen. That is the frame of mind in which to start, and if you succeed in cultivating it properly, you will know the real and fascinating joy of coming suddenly in the dusk upon the white blur of tents and the blaze of fires, and lo! here is everything safe and sound, the village headman salaaming to the ground and all the peons now full of a bustling activity, hammering lustily at a tent-peg which some unfortunate villager fixed with perfect precision hours before.

And here it occurs to the Civilian to wonder just what you imagine when you read the word "tents." Well, there were once upon a time a Collector and the Senior Major of a distinguished Regiment, and the Collector asked the Major to come into camp with him and do some shooting. The Major thought he had done enough camping in his time, but he was very fond of shooting, so he packed his *tent d'abri* or whatever it was and took the road. But when he came to the appointed place he found that the Collector had brought a canvas house for him, fourteen feet by fourteen, with a bathroom at the back, a veranda in front and a lordly roof many yards in height. This the Collector showed him with apologies, saying it was his small Swiss Cottage —if you thought that the only Swiss Cottage was in Finchley Road, you know little indeed of your Indian Empire—and when at dinner the Major beheld the Collector's tent he understood, for this was thirty feet long with dressing-rooms at each end and many doors and windows. The dinner was of seven courses and the Collector was angry because there were not eight. There was gin and vermouth and sherry and claret and whisky and Madeira and crème de menthe and benedictine and brandy and three different kinds of cheroots. On the following day's shoot they came at midday to a particularly lonely part of the country where there suddenly sprang out of a tank or a tope or a nadi or some such desolate place a swarm of myrmidons bearing iced beer and salad. The Major is said at this point to have become incoherent in his expressions and to have departed for home vowing that the camps of the Military and the Civil were indeed two different things.

From the Fable of the Soldier and the Sumptuous Civilian you will deduce the exact attitude of the English lady who is ready to share the dread hardships of camp towards her English sister who mustn't, couldn't and won't. The Civilian, at the risk of offending, must confess that—sickness and young children always excepted—he is not enamoured of the lady of the Six Months School who must be sent to the Hills for half the year and kept the other half in headquarters with a separate establishment, so that people meeting the man of the house in his ill-found camp say, "How the deuce does Stiggers manage to be so much in debt?" He will do her the justice to say that she is genuine; she really does believe she cannot possibly stand life in India. Perhaps her mother told her so at home; anyway she has never tried. The Civilian would feel more charitably towards her if she would even endeavour to see and enjoy the Hills when she gets there; but instead she sits in Clubs or goes in for a Plain Tale of sorts, and then, returning to headquarters for the cold weather, thwarts the good Major Vansuythen by the industrious manufacture of Station Rows. Why did she come out? The Civilian doesn't know. . . . With regard to the Sumptuous One, only remember if it seem to you that some of these things might have been done without, yet all the comforts in the world cannot do away with the stupefying heat of a tent when the temperature has passed a hundred, or the sodden discomfort of even the best-pitched tent in the rains. Moreover—and more especially in these depreciated times—not all Civilians are Sumptuous.

And here the Civilian would like to pause and unmask a thumping lie, a great fraud that has long been foisted upon credulous people, and that is the Indian climate. Anything bad that has been said about the Indian climate may stand; the Civilian wishes to attack the one good thing that has ever been attributed to it, and that is its dependability. There is a genial kind of Ass who is wont to observe that after all, give him the good old Indian climate; you know where you are with it. In the hot weather it will be hot, but bless our hearts, one at least knows that it *will* be hot and won't suddenly turn round and rain on you. Let us consider this assertion.

In December and January you can count that it will be fair and dry, but for the other ten months of the year there is no moment when you are not liable to see the sky change hurriedly from blue to black and to be drenched and dazed with a deluge out of the prehistoric era. Not very long ago, and in that month of May which is popularly supposed to be one long succession of blazing cloudless skies, the Civilian set out to change camp ; he walked from six in the morning until eight, and at the end of that time he fell into a chair like a limp rag, for the heat even at that hour of the morning was stifling. But he had not sat there half an hour when a cloud came over the shoulder of a hill, and before he knew it there came a roaring blast of bitter wind with a drive of solid water in it that sent all hands to the pegs and guy-ropes, and very nearly took the Civilian and his whole establishment by the board. As the Civilian wrestled with the tent-flaps there whizzed past him a bolt of lightning with the smash and roar of a cannon shot and something struck him keenly behind the ear and he found himself being battered by hailstones the size of marbles. Then the rain came down like a flood and rivers leapt off the hill in all directions and rushed gaily through the Civilian's tent so that he was obliged to set his dog upon a chair and his person upon his office table, wrapping himself in warm clothes to keep out the chill of the blast. And in two hours the sun was baking upon him again. It baked until sunset and it rose next morning and blazed till ten minutes to nine ; and at nine you could not see ten yards for a wall-like curtain of cold white mist that came down from nowhere and set the tent-ropes and eaves weeping in misery. The Civilian then sat down and wrote to a prominent member of the Genial Ass tribe to come into camp with him and test the dependability of the Indian climate in May. But it appeared that this person had already gone into camp and had trustfully pitched his tents in the shade of a dry tank-bed, and in the middle of the night a cloud burst on a neighbouring hill and the rains fell and the winds blew and beat upon that tank, and the last state of that man was worse than the first. So the Civilian thinks that the Dependable Climate must be another of the eccentricities of the North of India like Polo and Regimental Dances and Plain Tales from the Hills.

Nowadays there are so many Travellers' Bungalows in the ordinary district that the tents of our forefathers, like their horses, are becoming a thing of the past—though it goes without saying that your own nice tent is infinitely preferable to the poorer kind of Travellers' Bungalow which has a leaky roof, no punkah and many, many inhabitants. Travellers' Bungalows—*vide* Government Order—may be occupied at a cost of eight annas a day for a single person and twelve annas a day for a married couple; what the charge would be for a couple who announced that they were not married the Civilian has never been able to ascertain. If the Devil were to come to the Civilian and say to him, "Sell me your soul, and you shall instantly know all the stories of all Travellers' Bungalows and everything that has happened in them," the Civilian would succumb; for indeed to know that would be far more interesting than having a soul, and even if one kept one's soul after such knowledge it would be in such a state as to be of little service to any one. Hear Mr. Kipling on the subject—he calls them Dak-Bungalows, but it is all the same thing. "If a man said to a confirmed dak-bungalow haunter: 'There is a corpse in the next room, and there's a mad girl in the next one, and the woman and the man on that camel have just eloped from a place sixty miles away,' the hearer would not disbelieve, because he would know that nothing is too wild, grotesque, or horrible to happen in a dak-bungalow." Further, "Seeing that a fair proportion of the tragedy of our lives in India acted itself in dak-bungalows, I wondered that I had met no ghosts. A ghost that would voluntarily hang about a dak-bungalow would be mad, of course; but so many men have died mad in dak-bungalows that there must be a fair percentage of lunatic ghosts."

This is alarming to read, but the Civilian admits that it is nothing but the truth; and he will assert that it applies to all the older Travellers' Bungalows in Madras not less than in the north. There is nothing either but the passing of a little time in the way of its applying also to all these newer erections of brick and tile which stand up to-day so fair and fresh and practical and sane. The Civilian has slept in rooms which have told him in the watches of the night that they have seen men blow their brains out over that very table or die one or other of the horrible

Indian deaths in that very bed; and once on the Trunk Road he sojourned in a dreadful old place of many rooms and no comfort, yellow and discoloured by the rains of ages and washed over inside with a horrible deepish blue; and there, he learned, there had been two suicides—one of them a lady, which is rare—a very palpable and undoubted murder, and, subsequently, a man of sound constitution who had apparently died of pure fright. Now if you ask the Civilian what killed that man he will tell you that he saw a snake sitting on his bed and will brazen it out at that, for he has to live a good deal in Travellers' Bungalows and he is not going to start thinking about such matters. Strange, strange places are Travellers' Bungalows, and the Civilian does honestly believe that they contain within their plain and inornate walls more of the history of our people in India than any monument in the land. But that is a history which could only be written by one who had really sold his soul to the Devil and so found all things out; as it is, there they stand hiding and treasuring up in themselves the most wonderful and sinister stories in the world.

The Civilian has said that all camps with a very few exceptions are good; and so they are, but he would not have you believe that all camps are like those he has described so far. The greater part of British India being, by an error of the people who made the annexations, plains, it follows that the majority of camps will not be situated in anything deserving the name of scenery; and as, after all, one goes into camp to dispose of work which cannot be done at headquarters, it follows that one's lines must lie for the most part in civilized places. If the Civilian were asked to think of a typical camp he would figure to himself a grove of mangoes or coco-nuts somewhere by the side of a road, two white tents standing under the trees, the smoke and babel of the servants' tent somewhere behind, and a temporary shed or two of bamboo and palmyra-leaves to serve as stables and the like. (Having once camped under the proverbial banyan tree he will not figure himself in any such place again, for ten thousand million black ants invaded him in the night and he barely escaped with his life and his effects.) Up the road will be a little bare rocky and stony hill on the top of which it will be nice to sit and look about one; and down the road, half a mile or so away, will be a village; in the intervening space, some open pasture grounds with peaceable goats and buffaloes wandering thereon. In the morning before breakfast one can ascend to the summit of the little hill and see the smoke rising from the village and the women going out for water with their great brass pots on their heads; and in the evening one can climb up the same hill and watch the sunset and see the cattle coming in from the fields and the village tucking itself away for the night as the shadows come down. You who go out in the evenings to dinners and theatres turning the good and restful night into day, you cannot know the peacefulness of evening, the pleasant feeling of putting oneself into harmony with the set of the day, the agreeableness of the very unexciting knowledge that soon it will be dark and you will have your dinner and go to bed. The Civilian has often become so enamoured of the simple life that he has thought of building himself a little house of stone and thatch in some such place where he could sit on a hill in the mornings and evenings and sleep in the warm afternoons, this being so clearly what mornings and evenings and afternoons are for; but unfortunately he has always thought better of it, or some Philistine has come along and asked him with the coarse bluntness of Philistines on what he would propose to subsist.

"But, good Civilian, what is it you *do* in camp? Do you do nothing but climb hills and see sunsets?" Nay, masters, there are inspections. There are always inspections to be done everywhere and the purpose of one's going into camp is to do them. One inspects everything from Taluk Offices and Sub-Jails down to toddy-trees and field-boundaries. They are nearly all dreary, but most horrible of all is a kind of inspection known as *asmoish* or some such thing, which means going over fields where the crops have failed to see if the wretched owners are entitled to any remission of the revenue. It is a disgusting business, wandering along field-bunds—and falling off them every now and then into mud and water—the sun beating down on one's head while the karnam of the village and the Revenue Inspector fumble in imbecile confusion with maps and accounts. (No Indian can understand a map or find the place in a book.) So on and on while the karnam drops the accounts in the mud, and the Tahsildar quarrels with the clerk as to which map is which, and the Revenue Inspector, faint yet pursuing, babbles that in Number Two Hundred and Sixty-five D there was two anna crop of paddy on thirty cents and also seventy cents of dry-crop cholam grown on wetland and twenty-five cents of rain-fed gingelly; and you gaze and gape at where they tell you 265 D is and say "Yes, yes," and pass on. Schools are better than this, and would be better still if they were not housed in such appallingly stuffy buildings and if the pupils would not sing; for the Indian child can be very engaging, and indeed if India were entirely peopled by such children it would be a delightful place. The Civilian used to sit on a chair with garlands round his neck and flowers and fruits in his hands, looking no doubt no end of a fool, while some Juno-eyed little damsel explained to him the difference between a giraffe and a rhinoceros as portrayed on a painted card hung on the wall, or some sketchily clad young gentleman, consisting to the eye at least almost entirely of stomach, identified various objects which the Civilian displayed before his acute vision. . . . And if any one should say at this stage that to sit and make an idiot of himself among infants was the most suitable thing for the Civilian to do, he will esteem it a compliment and thank him very kindly.

In camp, too, one sees the Indian village as it was, is now and evermore shall be—a place where neither municipalities nor police do vex, nor preachers weary the ear with exhortations. It has a well—which is sometimes nearly dry—and it has a Rama-kovil where-at to perform its ceremonies, and it has a moneylender and a Hindu priest, and what more does it want? It is true that the well is insanitary, that the Rama-kovil is settling down with a list to port, and the money-lender charges twelve and a half per cent. and the priest is an old scoundrel; it is true that the streets are narrow and twisted, that the houses and huts stand about in no order but one on top of another, that there is no drainage of any sort, that cattle and refuse block the pathways, that there is no light in the place o' nights, and that in the rains everything is one glorious sea of mud scarcely penetrable to the ordinary human being. All this is so, and doubtless some of it is a trifle inconvenient, but it has always been so, any one but an idiot knows that people and villages are made like that, so what is the good of talking about it any more? After all, priests have a right to be villainous if they like, and the sowcar's interest is no greater than any other sowcar's; if the Rama-kovil falls down altogether some rich man will build it up again. As to streets and street-lamps and drains, who ever heard of such things; the rains fall once a year and surely that is washing-out enough for any reasonable being. You say there are disease and dirt in the houses and bad smells and no sanitation, but people as good as you lived here all their lives and died here and never took any harm, so there! The Civilian is a man of conservative soul and he sympathizes with all this thoroughly, but unfortunately Government have placed him in an anomalous position by insisting that these people want to be improved in spite of all that they themselves can say to the contrary. The task of bettering those who are perfectly pleased with themselves is not delightful, but a G.O. is a G.O., and so once more into the breach and let us hope that Heaven will approve of what we do, for no one seems likely to be pleased with it on earth.

In camp you meet the most interesting people in India. Besides the people of your own caste whom you meet with the stiffness of headquarters all worked out of them, you come upon the middle stratum and the lower stratum, and, best of all, the people who used to be the one and have become the other. You foregather with them in some remote wayside bungalow, you get one fascinating glimpse into the kind of life they lead, and then next morning your roads part and you never see them again. Perhaps that is just the secret of their attraction—that you are never going to see them again ; perhaps if you were to see them again they would become commonplace or offensive. It may be so, but it is delightful to meet them once in a way and so peep through the shutters into the life of that extraordinary section of humanity that lies between the two races, knowing everything and keeping its lips inexorably sealed. If one had the knowledge of these people one could begin to rule India and perhaps to understand it ; but the Civilian fears that if one were to achieve that state of wisdom one would have understood so much that one would be no longer in a fit state to rule anything.

And it is in camp, too, that one meets that type of Indian who has given the Oriental his reputation for urbanity—the man who is involved in a lifelong and thankless struggle with the soil, who has almost everything to complain of and yet rarely complains. He will come shyly to the door of your tent, bringing his friends with him and a little brass tray of offerings; he will fall at your feet, touching the ground with his head and calling upon you as upon a god. He will not force himself upon you, he will wait your pleasure, and when you have heard him he trusts you absolutely. Your clerk will laugh at him, but then your clerk has had an education: that trust is one of the compensations of India. Even now he is not what he was, this plain and simple villager, and he is growing scarcer and scarcer every day, but, oh, the comfort of coming among such people and getting away even for a little from the —well, from the others!

Why is he getting scarcer every day? Why isn't he preserved and cherished and treasured and nurtured and bred? The Civilian could tell you what he thinks are the reasons for these things also; but he would have you remember that he is writing harmlessly about camp and that he must not be encouraged to get on to controversial topics. These are Problems of Administration; and Problems of Administration would not interest you, and the Civilian does not really know anything whatever about them.

VI

THE SHIKAR COUNTRY

THERE must be a number of people who, having read what the Civilian has had to say about Camp, have come to the conclusion that suspicions they had been long harbouring were well-founded and that the Civilian is a hopeless lunatic. What else can one say about a man who writes about camping in India and apparently likes it, and yet says nothing about shikar? What is the good of going into camp if you are not going to shoot, and if you do not shoot what enjoyment can you possibly derive? Well, shikar is the quest of wild animals, the hunting of game, large and small—anything from rogue elephants to butterflies and beetles; but principally it refers to the tracking and destroying of the larger beasts—bison, tiger, bear, panther and deer.

The Civilian left it out of his description of camp with a purpose and he has no intention of writing anything whatever about it; it is a thing by itself and deserves to be so treated. Moreover, these memoirs are not written haphazard; they are being done in a sort of geographical progression and they have an aim and a goal in view. You are to observe that we began upon the Edge of India upon which we found the great and perplexing city of Madras; the consideration of Madras led us out into the mofussil headquarters and we found that these drove us into camp. We have worked inland through the ordinary camping districts and now we are going into the Shikar Country, which for the most part may be taken to mean the circle of foot-hills lying round the Mysore plateau and Haiderabad and the Nilgiri Hills. Presently, if anything like fortune attend us, we shall ascend these very Nilgiris themselves and then there will be no more to be said and we may die happy.

Please also to observe with care the title of this chapter; it is called "The Shikar Country," not "Shikar." The Civilian is a shikarri of the most amateur order, and it is not for him to flounder with inaccuracies and platitudes at the heels of the great Nimrods of the hunt. Moreover, unless to those who have their hearts in the game, the Book of Nimrod is often a lamentably tedious piece of work; it is frequently not too well written and possesses a charm only because the enthusiasm of the author shines through it like a burning light. The Civilian does not suppose that if he told you he had shot a sambhur with forty-inch horns, you would know whether this was longways or between the tips, or whether it was a good head or a bad; and he cannot suppose you are interested in the burning question of whether the bulk of a tiger should be treated as a rectangle and calculated on the product of the height and the length of the actual body, or whether it is a mere matter of length longways, tail and all. These are vital matters, but if they were to be elaborated here you would cry aloud "The Civilian is a bore," and cast him from you, which is what he is trying to avoid.

But the Shikar Country has to be considered, because it is a mistake to suppose that people are fond of shikar because they are fond of killing beasts. Even the most successful do not really kill so very many, and the score or so of skins and heads in Nimrod's bungalow represent countless long vigils of the night that were unrewarded save by the sweetness of the dawn, countless sums disbursed to beaters who beat nothing, many, many days of unsuccessful wandering. If Nimrod simply desired to hunt and kill, he would purchase a flock of goats, give them to his peons to hide in the nearest forest nicely tied to trees, and then he would go out and find them and kill them one after another. The most insane, however—and in India there have been some notable eccentrics—have never been known to attempt this. Nor does the Civilian think it is altogether a question of liking the jungle and the wild places, though that has much more to do with it. It is, he believes, at root the preference of meditation to conversation. Persons imbued with the passion for hearing their own tongues may go forth often and slay many animals, but they cannot be said to be true shikarris; they are not going out for the mere pleasure of doing it. They will be cross and ill-tempered if the pursuit has failed, whereas your true shikarri does not mind much either way. If you are going to have any chance at all, however, it is manifestly necessary that you hold your tongue—though the Civilian has heard of people who went to the expense and trouble of erecting a machân, and then had loud crashing soda bottles opened every hour or so beside them, and finally grumbled because they shot nothing.

Now no man will sit quite still unless he has to, and even then some—including the Civilian—cannot achieve it, but your devotee of meditation desires to sit still above all things, and though his own will cannot effect this absolute rigidity of posture, yet his will combined with the hope of the hunt may. And it is the Civilian's firm belief that it is the pleasure of meditation in the great silences and distances of the jungle country, the sitting quite perfectly still and thinking about anything that comes into your head, that draws its votaries to shikar far more than all the spots and stripes and horns and tushes that ever were. Very often they are not aware of it themselves; but it remains a fact that few great shikarris are brilliant conversationalists and few brilliant conversationalists are much distinguished in the chase. The Civilian's idea of shikar is to go out into the Shikar Country and meditate. He may be talking nonsense, but he has sometimes thought that if one can absolutely overcome one's body so that it becomes a mere block of substance, absolutely silent and absolutely still, one's spirit can get away from it and come into tune and touch with the place around one as do, no doubt, the spirits of animals. Every one can remember one or two quite ordinary places which for no special reason pleased extraordinarily, certain commonplace walks that were particularly joyous and delightful, a few days when one did nothing in particular and yet enjoyed things beyond belief: well, the reason was that for the time being he was in tune with his surroundings. He did not achieve it; it just happened so. But the Civilian has been told—and he believes it—that this is a thing which can be cultivated, and of all the places he has tried he has found it most easy to cultivate in the Shikar Country. It is a thing worth going on with, because if you could command it always you could always command happiness; but the Civilian never got much further than the inducing of a certain peacefulness of mind and a tantalizing sense of getting nearer to the heart of things than he had been before. That is what he means by the charm of the Shikar Country, and that is what took him there. "But did he ever shoot anything?" Yes—quite often.

The Cold Water School, here in their element, do not hesitate to affirm that there is no shikar to be got in the Madras Presidency anywhere, at any time, or by any conceivable means or exertions you care to employ. They further assert that the silent meditations of the Civilian induce nothing but acute malarial fever. The strength and weakness of this deplorable sect lies in the fact that its tenets are never less and never more than fractional truths; but this time the fraction approaches a little nearer to the integer than usual. There is no gainsaying the fact that nowadays game is remarkably hard to come by, and unless you have the luck which, according to the disappointed, favours fools you may seek long and wearily and find nothing. It is therefore all the better if you are a true shikarri and can take it as a game and play it for its own sake. Indeed, unless you are to look at it this way, you had better, in the Madras Presidency, leave shikar alone. It is also true that in the Shikar Country you frequently run the risk of contracting fever, and if you choose to regulate your affairs like an idiot, and sit about with portions of your person exposed and sleep under bushes and neglect your commissariat, you stand an excellent chance of being left in the Shikar Country till the Day of Judgment. It goes against the Civilian's grain to have to admit so much of truth in any of the doctrines of the Cold Water School, but he does so admit it in order that his other fulminations against them may carry the more weight.

The Civilian's first shooting in India was not done in the Shikar Country at all, but was of the low-ground variety so beloved of many—snipe and duck. He went out with a Superior and the Superior's Friend; the Superior was rather kind to him, but the Friend, who talked very large indeed, apparently regarded him as a dangerous lunatic who should not have been entrusted with firearms. It relieved the Civilian greatly when he himself shot six snipe which included a jack and a painter, and the Superior's Friend shot nothing at all. This Fable of the Civilian and the Depreciatory Friend is recorded merely as a warning against talking at large when your eye may be out, as the Civilian has no doubt that the Friend was really a far better shot than he. There are men who would gladly hang him for saying it, but the fact is that the Civilian finds snipe shooting in India a trifle tedious and very exhausting; it may mean ploughing through mud and water up to your ankles, your knees, or sometimes your waist; and the surroundings are commonly of that Fititis-inspiring type germane to Delta Districts. It is also very difficult—remember the Civilian writes as a novice—to know what is a genuine snipe and what is a jack or a painter or a horrid kind of squeaking plover that is more like a snipe than either. The Civilian was only able to invent one rule: if anything rises in such a way as to give you a reasonably decent shot at it, then it is not a snipe. This is infallible and he recommends it.

Contrary to reputation the Indian snipe and duck are very often terribly wild, and have to be stalked like deer. The Civilian has a memory of many mornings in wet places with a blinding light coming back off the water, when he lay flat in a sort of punt or dug-out or anything he could get and was pushed along by some faithful creature crawling in the mud and water behind. The duck would all be sitting in a reedy corner like so many corks, very hard to see in the bad light; and at the right moment—if they didn't go off first—they were put up and the Civilian would miss them lavishly. For this he was not altogether to blame, as that pestilent fellow the village shikarri had made them uncommonly wary and they turned and rose and ducked in the twinkling of an eye. A better way was to get into the boat and lie up in the rushes, but even at that it was long odds that they got wind of one somehow and took any road but that which would lead them near one's position. They went up, too, like biplanes. They were just like English duck, indeed they were English duck—teal, pintail, pochard and the rest with very little difference. It is, by the way, a curious fact that the local of Indian or partial Indian descent seems utterly unable to tell the difference between duck and any other waterfowl: the Civilian once went out shooting with a very good friend of his who was an Indian and the friend returned a bag of one tern, one greenshank, two water-hens, a dove, a grebe, and an appalling monstrosity which science has never identified to this day. The Civilian, however, need not speak; for once in his early days he found a new kind of duck, rather large and tame and easy to shoot: he was pleased with this and shot several and brought them back to the camp in great glee. But, unfortunately, they were not duck and the Civilian has still to live down that episode among those who know.

All this sort of thing, however—the tanks with old temples mouldering among the reeds, the paddy-fields and the sticky black mud and dazzling water—has nothing to do with the Shikar Country and has to be left behind when you enter it. There is no pen yet which has been able to give the real effect of these lone and delicious places, though many have come near enough to make fine reading; and so the Civilian has little faith in his own and will not put it to the test, lest he be shamed and fail miserably. He will simply tell you then that there are hills; but they are different from other hills, for they are no two of them alike and they possess an uncanny sort of life and stand about and over you like so many personalities, mostly rather frightening and uncivil. Over and around these is jungle of all sorts and colours—scrub, thorn and tree, with dense clumps of bamboo into which you could not push your way if you tried—and here and there, just to remind you you are in India, a seedling palm looking very timid and uncomfortable. Wandering about by paths that never were made by man, you will look into innumerable quiet valleys full of sunshine, and down them to more and more peaks of hot stone; and everywhere, buried in the jungle or balanced beautifully on the sky-line, are great boulders and slabs and pillars of immemorial rock. Here and there you will come upon basins and pits in the hills which you enter by a narrow crack and must leave by that same way, for there is no other; and, strangest of all, you will find odd blocks and fragments of timeless masonry, which surely none but devils could have built. With these be wary, for though the devils may have left them snakes will certainly remain.

Sometimes in the midst of this dry and sun-scorched wilderness you will be gifted with streams of running water, purring down over the soft grey rock in the shade of enormous trees, and here you may sit for a while in the chequered twilight and watch the bright dragon-flies darting hither and yon and soothe yourself with the sweet scents of unknown flowers and the threshing-mill drone of innumerable bees. You will hear the wailing of gigantic and banshee cats, which are really peacocks; and the sound of steamers' sirens very deep and mournful, which is done by a black and brown bird with a long tail; and all round you spirit-voices will say "No luck, no luck," and "Have a drink, have a drink," for which derision and advice you are indebted in truth to the little portly consequential jungle-fowl. Presently when your mind has become attuned to wonder and your eyes a little strained by the sun over wide spaces, you will see strange portents; monsters will thrust their heads at you from the thickets, boulders on the sky-line will take the form of gigantic bears, and such deer as never were known to mortal man will appear to you upon the hillsides. Meanwhile you will see the cloud-shadows chasing one another along the mountains, and far away the thunder will growl and mutter angrily at your intrusion, and every pathway and patch of earth will be marked with the comings and goings of the peoples who hold no dealings with man. There will be a total stillness; you will walk on the thick sand of a river-bed or a forest path without sound; you are in an enchanted land and at any moment the most unusual things might begin to happen.

One goes to the Shikar Country mostly in the

early part of the hot weather—the end of March or April, for then the drinking-pools have become few in number and the lords of the jungle, having been cursed with thirst to their destruction, must come down to a given place to slake it. India is a hot country, as there is no denying; but when it becomes hot in earnest there is no sense in sitting down and watching the thermometer; it is better to go out and chase Papilio Hector—who will always oblige—round and round the compound, so that you may be properly wearied and rest at your appointed times. And if, when you come to your nightly pallet, you find that it has just been taken out of an oven and is a shade distasteful, do not go and sit in a long chair and drink whisky; take to yourself a rifle and a man to show the way and sally you forth to some moonlit jungle pool, and sit there as still as you can. It is more than probable that nothing will come near; but there is always the expectation, and now and then a fusillade of frogs diving into the pool on some false alarm to give you hope; and you may at all events listen to the jungle noises round about you—the ill-tempered ravings of the nightjars, the cranes explaining to you in measured sentences the extreme weariness of life, the velvet swoop of a contemptuous owl. You may watch the slow march of the odd-looking Indian constellations above your head; and it will be strange if by midnight you do not feel you can face your bed after all. The Civilian remembers one such night at a place where a great rock hill drew in the heat all day and blasted it forth again like a furnace all night; when, after sitting in a cold bath for an hour on end and wading through a dinner he did not in the least want, he felt that he was upon the point of death. He did not die, however, but having heard that a panther had come down a week back and taken a dog he purchased instead from the village a piebald kid, which he took out and tied up under a tree at the foot of the hill. He then climbed up into the tree and sat there and amused himself by watching Arcturus passing one branch after another; the kid meanwhile, having decided that it was in no great danger, fell asleep and snored thunderously. Having meditated thus for some hours on all manner of great subjects and the panther not appearing, the Civilian came to the conclusion that the kid had more sense than he had and, descending, went back to his bed, where he slept perfectly well till seven.

It is not to be supposed that one goes into the Shikar Country alone, and indeed one of the charms of the business is the curious succession of varied companions upon whom you are intimately thrust by the immensity of your surroundings for hours or days at a time. Always, of course, one has one or more native shikarris; these are to be distinguished from their fellows by their extreme hideousness and by a skinniness which approaches towards hallucination. The Civilian cannot remember ever having seen one over five feet high, and they look as if the first blast of wind would carry them away over the nearest mountain; yet it takes a man in the very pink of condition and training to keep up with them on a long day's hunt—one of those cruel days when one hits the creature first at six in the morning and kills it finally after all manner of exertions ten miles away at four in the afternoon. The shikarri will go through this without a tremor—and that too after he has been sitting up somewhere all night; but you will be a sorry sight at the end of it. Their capacity for work seems to increase slightly the more hideous and emaciated they are; but when it comes to the lore or knowledge of shikar they are as a general rule—this refers to the ordinary village shikarri—very nearly useless, telling innumerable lies and speaking of that about which they know nothing. For all this, however, it is these wretches, armed with a condemned Police carbine or an old double-barrel or a country musket of a type unknown to modern makers, who kill off the game and spoil the Indian shikar. And trust them not at all. There was once a young Policeman and a tiger and a station dinner on Christmas Eve. The Policeman thought he would rather have the tiger than the dinner, so about three in the morning when his friends were just going to their beds he got out of his and went out to the kill. The tiger came and went, but in the interval the Policeman got in a very good shot and, he was convinced, hit it. This, however, the shikarris with one voice denied, and the Policeman, being fresh from home and having not yet realized—it takes a time to realize—the meanness of the Oriental mind on occasion, went home without either the tiger or the dinner. As a matter of fact, the tiger was all but dead, and the shikarris, having accepted the Policeman's largesses with many salaams, tracked it down in twenty minutes, polished it off with a lethal bullet stolen from the Policeman for that purpose, and disposed of it in the proper quarters with great profit to themselves. To the Fable of the Green Policeman there are two morals at least: in the first place, until you have learned do not trust yourself to people of unsporting instincts; and, in the second, in India, pay on sight only and then by results.

But the Civilian is not here to tell tales of shikar, so he will omit the stories of X's remarkable accuracy in shooting the kill or how Y after a long and weary day bagged a fine domestic buffalo which had wandered from some village; let us back to our companions of the Shikar Country and find the Civilian's good friend Mr. Gopala Rao, subordinate Forest Official, " mobbilizing his farces " for a beat. Here is a man who is nothing if not Nimrod. Great, genial, bellowing, perspiring idiot, how the Civilian wishes you could meet him; he would change all your ideas of India in ten minutes. Beside Mr. Gopala Rao, Baron Munchausen was a tyro and Ananias hid his head for very shame. The Civilian still remembers how they sat amicably on the back of an elephant going along a wooded road between hills in a pouring deluge of rain, while that great man, undeterred by the weeping heavens, explained with illustrations the difference between Telugu and Tamil music—knowing nothing, as the Civilian afterwards discovered, about either; and thereafter how he charmed the ear with a series of anecdotes of the chase so astounding that the Civilian had much ado to retain his seat. And again how he persuaded this inexperienced enthusiast to assemble a vast horde of beaters and spend three-quarters of a day beating up and down a hill which, as the Civilian now sees, could have contained nothing more noble than a porcupine. And yet again how with much stage-whispering and mystery, he led the Civilian to a cave and told him there was a panther inside, and how, after shouting and gesticulating freely in front of the place for some time, he lost patience and discharged his gun into the cave and solemnly assured the Civilian that in five minutes the animal would emerge. Dear fellow! his was a simple heart; and the Civilian would give much to possess that unfaltering trust in your credulity which Mr. Gopala Rao placed in his.

If you have read any books on shikar you will of course be aware that the proper people with whom to go forth on these expeditions are Rajas; and so they are, for if the Raja cannot find game and levy an army of beaters it is a sad look-out. The Civilian, however, cannot give you any accounts of shikar in these high circles, for he never went out with a Raja, though he has some experience of zamindars, which is the next best thing. The only real and titular Raja of his acquaintance belonged to the old school and could just climb into the reception-room on the second storey of his palace; he then became breathless and drank brandy. But the Civilian knew a zamindar who delighted in the pleasant sport of coursing blackbuck and antelope with half-tamed cheetahs, the interesting moment of this pastime coming in when one had to pull the cheetah off his quarry. This zamindar also found tiger-shooting dull, so he netted and speared them. This is absolutely and strictly true. It is, moreover, related of him that, one of his elephants going *musth*—that is to say, dangerously and homicidally mad—he went into the jungle after it on its stable companion and caught it single-handed and brought it back. As to this, however, the Civilian will not swear. As a contrast to this there was another zamindar with whom the Civilian once went forth to shoot, who behaved less gallantly; for he asked the Civilian on some transparent pretext to ride on in front, and when the Civilian looked round, behold his host, having been hoisted into the saddle by a groom, was having his horse led along by the head. In the evening he refused to go out shooting as he had promised, and the Civilian, becoming annoyed at being offered falsehoods which would not have deceived an infant, went out unexpectedly and discovered his host sitting in his shirt watching a cock-fight. But all kinds go to make a world; and to prove this the Civilian fell in, a week or two later, with a most sporting and gentlemanly chieftain on the Haiderabad border who owned a garden containing seventy-two different kinds of roses and a tope with eighty-eight varieties of mango; and his son gave the Civilian a lesson on one side of Indian character. The son, whose eyes were most beautifully brightened and done-off with lamp-black, rode a huge ramping piebald countrybred with a rusty iron bit and a snaffle very much patched and worn. In open country nothing would induce him to indulge this animal in more than a trot, but no sooner did they come to a village than he clapped in his spurs and dashed headlong down the street like a whirlwind scattering the population, human and animal, on all sides. It was magnificent; but the Civilian, having held his horse in over all these miles of open country and knowing quite well that its feet were *not* countrybred, felt that it was scarcely war.

The Shikar Country when a proprietor of sporting instincts has done his worst with it is an extraordinary sight, as the Civilian was once privileged to see. Being invited to shoot on a certain estate, he was driven in a two-horse carriage into the most maniacal country he ever beheld. In the heart of the wilderness stood a palatial bungalow, and from this there radiated in all directions huge broad motor roads, charging through the jungle as straight as a die and taking no heed of obstacles of any sort. At the further end of these were little tanks on the banks of which stood such towers as any freebooter of the older school would have called a castle—tremendous erections of brick and chunam, two stories high and with rooms at the back. In these, instead of the customary cot in a tree, one sat up for such creatures as might come to the tank to drink. Now on a May night a tiny room six feet high in the roof at most and with infinitesimal windows is not the most pleasant place to cohabit with an unwashed shikarri who has been exerting himself prodigiously, but, on the other hand, one could hold the place against every charging panther in South India. The Civilian was motored about and given champagne and the run of these martello towers; but it is not every panther that charges and it is not every man who is charged by a panther who perishes; and so, all things considered, the Civilian thinks that he prefers a modest whisky-and-soda and the quiet peace of the jungle paths and a machân built up among the cool and scented leaves.

The Civilian will now tell a terrible secret about himself: it is that he collects butterflies. It is regarded as just a little indecent in India to collect butterflies; indeed, unless perhaps one were to collect eggs, there could be nothing much worse. It is a Eurasian sort of thing to do. Nathless the Civilian defiantly maintains that it is a very excellent and beneficial pursuit, because it takes one out in the sun and air when otherwise one would not go. It gives one two things very necessary in India—exercise and an interest outside one's work; if you doubt the exercise, try ten rounds with Helen or Paris or one of those light-winged fellows in yellow and black on a steep hillside with insecure going underfoot. You may be in a place which has never been blessed with tiger, sambhur, blackbuck, pig, duck, snipe or pigeon; but there is no place in India that is not blessed in some measure with butterflies. The Shikar Country is the best place to get them, of course, on the baking gravelly slopes at the hillfoots, by the flowering bushes along the jungle highways, by the river-bed pools, or when they go like emerald and sapphire suns in the dusk of a fern-hung grotto under a fall. You must go out into the sun, for that is where the butterflies go who have more sense than you, and the sun will be hot, but in reason it will do you nothing but good. All English ladies in India—who never see the sun, which, as every one knows, was designed for the sole purpose of putting colour into their cheeks—should be forced to chase butterflies for one hour daily—ten to eleven in the cold weather and nine to ten in the hot. It is a perfectly graceful procedure and it would do them no end of good; for the Civilian does verily believe that if ladies would desist from burying themselves in the twilit depths of bungalows all day long there would be no Six Months School in India at all. They will get some that will reward any one with an eye for colours—Sarpedon who is tinted like a late November sunset with a touch of frost in it, Polymnestor who has been to both Oxford and Cambridge and wears both blues impartially, Hector who still carries the blood-stained uniform of the Trojan army, and Polites a man about town in the most faultless evening dress. Now these are wise words of the Civilian's; but nobody will take any notice of them.

To write about the Shikar Country is a hard task; see what a hash the Civilian has made of it. One knows so clearly what it is and how one feels about it, and yet one lacks utterly the words to describe. "Rock hills," "jungle," "forest"—that is all there is and the words convey nothing at all. The Hindu, who is a wise fellow and knows how many are the things which cannot be expressed, has devised a tale of a wonderful garden, wherein the happy visitor tasted and knew all the delights that earth can afford—which, contrary to common belief and appearance, were many ; but as he made to come out by the gate, in order that he might call and bring thither all his friends, an old man sitting there rose up and looked him keenly in the face so that although when he got outside he could still remember what he felt in the garden he could not describe or explain it to any one. The Civilian does not profess to know what or where was the garden that the Hindu author meant, but he thinks that such an old man as he of that garden must keep ward over the gates of the Shikar Country and, looking them in the eye, must seal the lips of those who visit it. At any rate he has sealed the Civilian's. All that will come into his head are phrases about the evening light on long, long vistas of green and purple hills, or the moon shining into tiny silver clearings in the jungle with the black darkness of Erebus hemming them all round like a wall, or the delicious peace that comes with watching the forests going to sleep at night; and if you think that these convey in any measure the impression at which he is driving let him tell you once and for all that they most lamentably do not. The old man at the gate has got him and there is no sense in fighting against magic.

So the Civilian is obliged to say now what he should have said at the beginning of the chapter and so saved us all trouble—that these are places to see and try for oneself. And so when you come to India, as all good people should do—it is quite true that the Wise Men came away from the East, but remember they had been there—you are to call upon the Civilian in the *mamul* and regulation suit of dark blue, and he will take it off and give you decent garments and set you upon a horse and take you away and away into the jungle. In the forenoon you shall sit with him in a shady place while the tormenting roar and clamour of the beat draws nearer and nearer; at midday he will give you beer and you shall rest under a great tree; at evening you shall halt upon a hill-top and look out upon that country of little wooded mountains which has neither beginning nor end; and at night you shall sit beside a pool in the moonlight and watch the distant lightning playing behind a curtain of cloud and see the universe roll over you and on. Then you will go away again. It is almost probable that you will have seen no sport, it is quite possible that you may not have liked it at all; but this much you will have gained—that you need never again disturb your mind with unavailing writers like the Civilian who try to describe the Shikar Country.

VII

THE AGENCY

THE Agency is the name that is given to a very large, indeed an enormous, stretch of hill and jungle country lying at any level from five hundred feet to five thousand which comes on in the three northernmost districts of the Madras Presidency. It is quite possible that there is some reason why this place should be called the Agency, but the Civilian could never find any one who could explain it to him and he is unable therefore to make it clear to you. Why these lands should not be ordinary districts and divisions, and how the great British Raj was ever so sensible as to take possession of such unusually pleasant places—these also be things withheld from our knowledge. The Agency does not strictly speaking come into that beautiful geographical progression towards the celestial hills which has been outlined as the scheme of this work, but it is worth a digression, and the Civilian must tell of it because a small bit of its fringe was once his. Of this small bit he will be understood to speak and he wishes with all his heart it could have been more. Not many people get to the Agency and those who do not are the losers.

The Agency was left out of the Shikar Country only for the reason that it is a place where one goes officially with work to do, and is not therefore beset with the lively magic of holidays. There is as much shikar, however, as any reasonable being could desire. There are great rivers in the more remote parts with vast swampy water-meadows, and there you may come upon the wild buffalo whose horns may be four feet long and who will charge you at sight; and in the grass-covered hills of the higher jungles there will be the gaur or bison which is not at all like any bison you ever saw, but is said by some to be the finest hunting in India. There are also sambhur and spotted deer and panthers and tigers and a few bears. The Civilian has foregathered with all these creatures, and can tell how one morning, as he was going through very long grass in a very thick fog, the earth suddenly burst into bison on all sides of him as a herd that had been lying down got up and bolted for the hills, and one very fine old bull who was in charge stood and stamped his foot at the Civilian and gave him clearly to understand his utter insignificance. And another time he came to what is called a salt-lick—a piece of sour earth on the bank of a stream where the animals take their medicine—and there, huge as a castle and black as Lucifer, he saw a solitary bison bull, and was awed by it for a good half minute before he knocked it flat on its side with a bullet not half an inch long and went home marvelling at the wonders of man's invention. Now the gaur—that is another name for the bison—are the real kings and rulers of the Agency, and it is a place far more suited to them than to human beings, yet a race of human beings of a curious sort has chosen to try to live there, and that is why fortunate and deserving Civilians are sometimes posted to these tracts.

Once you go to the Agency you must give up any idea of Indian scenery altogether. The Civilian has seen there places that resemble his conception of Thibet or the Caucasus, he has seen boggy uplands and hillocks just like those one finds on the north side of the Grampians and long quiet valleys something like the Yorkshire dales; and he has seen there the very noblest mountains that raise their great green shoulders clear of all forest or jungle with bare and towering cliffs of grey and black rock; but anything remotely resembling India he has never come across at all. It is true that the whole place is overrun and carpeted with the dwarf date-palm, but it rises only to a height of eighteen inches or so and from any distance gives the effect only of coarse grass—and worse than the coarsest of grass and the rankest of weeds it is, for it is tough as a hempen rope and the labour of man will hardly clear it from the ground it has made its own. The very palms have ceased to be the coco-nuts and palmyras and have become sago-palms which look like a cross between a palm and a blue gum and are altogether strange and disconcerting to the eye.

In all his wanderings in his Agency—which were not few—the Civilian saw nothing in the least like India except once, when he came suddenly in the bight of a hillside upon a very wet and prosperous village, and there in the middle of a country something like a heatherless Speyside, there was an astonishing hundred yards or so of sub-tropical scenery. There were tree-ferns and wild plantains and coffee bushes and great wet rice-fields and plots of saffron; and the huge shining butterflies of the lower hills wheeled lazily under the mangoes, and the very villagers looked a shade different and more civilized. Out of this as out of a dream, one rose on to a hillside as bare as a board, a great clear peak picked out with rocks and dwarf date and thorn-bushes going up to the five thousand foot line; and a grey Scotch mist swept into one's face and announced that no such things as tree-ferns and butterflies could ever have been. All along the paths were beautiful scented bushes, and in them sat the cicalas singing away with the regular swing of coolies hauling on a rope; and on the other side of the valley a stream came down from a shola of bigger trees and spread and trickled through some wet cultivation and dropped forty feet over a smooth grey rock.

The heroines of novels were always struck by the brilliance of the Indian colours; now even in the Plains, as the Civilian may have shown, India is not so bright as she is painted and in the Agency she is not bright at all; for the colours there are greys and greyish-greens with a thin wash of Prussian blue over all on hot mornings and sometimes in the evenings a glow of dull orange. It is a magnificent country, it is a country for kings and princes, a country worthy of the great regal gaur and the ten-foot man-eating tigers, but—it is not in any way India.

That this is so there are many and diverse signs—over and above any mere question of appearances. The first of these is that the ordinary Indian will not approach within five miles of it; he regards it with an awe and shuddering which if he would but transfer it to his Government would make the task of that long-suffering body comparatively light. He is simply terrified for it. From the highest in the land down to your butler and your cook, only the direst exigencies, the most appalling threats, or the most tempting largesses will persuade them to cross the Agency's fearful threshold. When Mr. Ramaswami Naidu, the Tahsildar, desires to paint any place in colours more than normally sable or to show that its general duress and arduousness are extreme, he calls it "worse than Agency." Announce that you are about to travel in the Agency and the urgent and leave-compelling mortalities among your servants' relatives become nothing short of wholesale; Sub-Magistrates and such people will go on their knees to avoid it; peons, clerks and mahouts blench at the order for an Agency camp. This they put down, if you be so foolish as to remark on it, to a dread of Agency fever, and Agency fever is a very bad form of malaria and a very actual and present curse.

But the researches of great men in the last thirty years have shown that this fever can be avoided to a very considerable extent ; yet the terror of the Agency does not diminish. There is therefore something more. Now the Civilian has previously stated that he is ready to believe in devils and has sometimes been made to believe in them altogether ; and his theory is that there are devils in the Agency who hate the people of the Plains and that the Plains people know it and fear the Agency accordingly. They realize that it is not their land, that it is strange and hostile to them and their country, that it is something outside ordinary India and that within its borders the ordinary Indian is a stranger and accursed. The unfortunate thing is that the Agency devils do not seem to object to Europeans who would appear to understand and propitiate them ; and in spite of all that anxious subordinates and advisers can do or say these mad fellows clamour for the Agency with one accord. They have come, one is given to understand, from homes of wealth and culture, they have taken the trouble to pass an arduous examination which might well entitle them to subside somewhere in peace for the rest of their natural lives, they are given riches and bungalows in the Plains with fine roads whereon to travel and fat safe villages wherein to camp ; yet they scorn these things as if they were of no account, and with a minimum of comforts—you cannot carry tons of luggage in the Agency—and a cramped and inadequate tent, they joyously parade and wander in these unhallowed regions on every available day of the year. Instead of sighing with relief and pouring coco-nut water on the head of any forbearing god they may still possess, they greet the news of a transfer from these regions with oaths and lamentations; and one being posted to an Agency Division writes home as though he had been advanced a grade. This, then, surely is a sign that the Agency is not as other parts of Hind—that to live in it is positively delightful to the European and to the Indian a positive horror.

Come now to the Agency people and consider again vast and sundering differentiations. Astounding as it may seem within at least the geographical bounds of India, the vulgar in the Agency (*a*) do not lie and (*b*) do not appreciate or esteem the value of money. They are a dwarfed and crushed and emaciated people, beaten down by the ravages of fever, by constant struggling with a captious climate and an unrewarding country, by the terror of wild beasts that prowl in the night, and by long, long years of hopeless interbreeding and wastage of stock. Their ideas are not numerous and their minds are slow in the last degree, but as they are simple, so they are honest. You may leave your tent standing unguarded at a point for days without troubling to pack the smallest of your things and when you return there will be nothing missing. He would be a confident man—or a very foolish—who would try this experiment in the Plains. A few years ago they would have run away at the sight of you—some of them will to this day. If a man of the Agency has done murder and is caught and brought before you, he does not call in a vakil and his wife's relations and concoct an elaborately unconvincing alibi; he tells you that the deceased was a swine and that he slew him accordingly, and his whole defence will be to impress you with the utter objectionableness of the victim and the entire impossibility of putting up with him any longer. The first time that this happened before him the Civilian—who had been a Magistrate in the Plains for a year or two before—nearly fell from the seat of judgment; he had actually gone so far as to start an order acquitting the accused but recovered himself in time. The relief of the line "Yes, I did it, but you would have done it yourself under the circumstances" after long years of "Your honour, I am a man of spotless integrity and never harmed a soul and the whole thing is a concoction got up by two men whom I in my virtuous way reported to Government for an offence"—the relief, the Civilian says, was so immense that only his iron sense of justice prevented him from there and then absolving the prisoners and presenting them with a testimonial and a purse of rupees.

The sad aspect of this desirable state of affairs is that it applies even already in a much less marked degree than it did twenty years ago; and there is no conceivable reason to doubt that in the course of time, as education advances and the Agency Tracts become more and more exploited and improved, it will die out altogether and the people of the Agency will lie and cheat with anybody. The Civilian hopes that before the dawning of that evil day he will have retired and become a Club bore in Piccadilly or an object of pity at some seaside resort or a distinguished golfer at Bedford—one of these three things, as all know, being the ultimate fate of all retired Civilians. (That is why they never retire until they are forced to, and then come back and buy land at Coonoor.) But perhaps in that day the devils who have sat in guard over the Agency may go away, and the people of the Plains having ceased to fear and hate it may come rushing in to enjoy it; and so some one at any rate may be pleased.

The Civilian has said that in the second place the people of the Agency cannot realize the value of money, and this, if you will but consider an instant, is perfectly natural also. Animals have no money and no need for it; and it is much the same with the villagers of the Agency whose lives have been set by a kind and merciful Providence very nearly upon the animal level. In the Agency a man could once live for sixpence or eightpence a month—six or eight shillings a year, think of it!—and every man owns or cultivates (or neglects) his little plot of land, every twentieth man has a cow or a buffalo or a couple of ploughing bullocks or a fowl or two. The natural result is that in the Agency, apart from the produce that goes down the ghats to be sold, nothing has any market value at all. The Civilian's supplies for a week cost about half-a-crown; chickens were a penny, eggs a penny halfpenny a dozen, milk nominal and firewood free. For carrying your luggage you paid a man fourpence whether he carries it twenty miles or two; and the loads that these walking skeletons will take over the most trying country—and take quickly—would surprise you.

Now this total lack of money values is not altogether a good thing, for where there is no desire for increase a man will do no more than he need, and the need of the Agency man, as has been said, is exceedingly small. Therefore he does not desire to heap up riches wherewith to pay his expenses and therefore he will not work unless he is inclined. And he is practically never inclined. Take a coolie of the Plains, give him a load to carry for half a day and fine him half his wage because instead of bringing it directly he sat down in toddy-shops and arrived hours late; he will pester and whine and grovel for an hour on end and nothing but physical violence will finally remove him. But your man of the Agency having similarly carried his load has to be practically tied down till the money is put in his hand to prevent his wandering away without it, and if the amount be short or even refused *in toto* he will wander away just the same. He grows his coffee on the high levels with great labour and trouble to himself; he carries it down on *jaddis* to the little ghat-foot market-town in the sweat of his brow, and there he comes in contact with the down-country trader's agent, who is to the shark what the shark is held to be towards more amiable fish. He sets out to sell his coffee by the maund at a price reasonable in the extreme and he knows perfectly well what a maund is, but the agent tells him that what he has brought is only half a maund and the incredible idiot hands it over, pockets the half price that the agent forces upon him, and toils away home up the ghat. Now these are the actions of simple and delightful folk; granted, but when it comes to working among them what, in the name of all the pastoral gods, is a man to do?

Nothing would be so bad if it were not for the characteristic which most distinguishes the Agency man from his fellows, and that is a hopeless and absolute apathy. Now the villager of the Plains, the ordinary ryot cultivator of the fields, could not possibly be described as energetic or enterprising, but his counterpart in the Agency carries this spirit of sleepy indifference to a pitch which can have few equals on the face of the round globe. He does not want to do anything, he does not care about anything, he does not value or seek or aspire to anything—which is a shade trying when your ostensible object is the reformation of him and his country. He does not much mind whether he lives or dies. The Civilian has seen an Agency coolie go down with heart failure after carrying a heavy load of mangoes up a ghat, and the man crawled to a pool of water and lay down and died aimlessly in the most disinterested and casual way. It was horrible. No one paid the slightest attention to him or worried about him in any way, but in the face of his own complete indifference this was perhaps excusable. With this example in view you will not expect to hear that the Agency peoples show a quick interest in clearing jungle for cultivation, building roads or setting up sanitary houses for themselves or others; and, indeed, they do not. If ever there was a consistent exponent of the Mantalini doctrine of life it is the man of the Agency; except that he has hardly the energy to regard the succession of things as damnable or as anything in particular at all. Everything is a trouble to him and too much trouble; if a tiger kills in his village and your camp is a mile away he will not come to tell you; although he does not at all approve of tigers and sincerely wishes them destroyed. He will not send his children to school even if you practically pay them to go by a system of universal prizes. If you try to talk to him about his condition he will run away and hide—in which perhaps he has the Civilian's sympathy, for the Civilian himself does not like to be talked to about his condition, especially by strangers. He raises his crops and sells his poor produce somehow because he has a sort of conviction that these are things it is impossible to avoid; if he thought he could give them up he would instantly. How it is that he does not starve or die of sheer inertia is a problem science has yet to solve.

It is here that the interbreeding comes in disastrously. For all the time that living man can remember—and certainly long before also—that fearsome line which separates plain from Agency has been overstepped by neither side. (It is a line that exists going round the place like a snake, and in places you can see it where it happens to be the cleared line of a forest reserve, and at the sight of that line, even from the safe side, peons and servants are smitten instanter with acute malarial fever.) Well, then, if the Plains fear the Agency, the Agency's mistrust of the Plains—not unfounded—amounts to a positive terror. At the head of the ghats that go down to the market-villages you will see a small cairn of stones with a larger pointed stone rising on end out of it; and if you watch those returning from the sale of their merchandise you will observe that they do obeisance to this stone in passing. It is a god—or more probably a goddess, the Agency is full of goddesses under a sort of general tutelage of the great Gangamma—and it receives the salaam of thanksgiving because it has brought back its votary in safety from the deadly peril of the Plains.

Agency people do not marry into the Plains nor they of the Plains into the Agency. And as the nomadic bands of Khonds and suchlike peoples who traffic about the countryside from time to time, migrating here and there for reasons no man clearly knows, are exclusive bodies in this respect, the men and women of the same little circle of villages are left to intermarry again and again. Thus the stock is reduced to a minimum of value, and this value those gentle creatures further proceed to lower by means of drink. An Agency man can drink anything, but he chiefly delights in vile arracks and toddys produced from the sago-palm and the *mohwa* tree—that tree of the pretty scented flowers whose early blossoming brings the early rains. The Civilian has in his mind one village over which he was once privileged to hold jurisdiction, which was known as the Village of Mangoes. Mangoes there may or may not have been, but it is a certain fact that a beneficent Creator had placed just at the back of it a colossal forest of sago-palms; and at the appropriate season of the year one would not find more than one-eighth of the male population of that place anything approaching sober. The Civilian can well remember one sixteen-mile march where he caught up upon his luggage load by load and beside each load at either end of the *jaddi*-pole there lay two figures prone, unconscious, clasping empty gourds in their hands, hopelessly and totally drunk. Whereupon the Civilian reviled his Government for that they stinted him in elephants, these being wise and profitable beasts and not given to strong waters.

The third great way in which the Agency differs from the Plains is the character of the work one must do there. Some time perhaps the Civilian will tell more closely what ordinary routine work in India is like—that absolutely undistinguished and mechanical grind in which two-thirds of all the services perforce must spend their days; and then you will realize what a godsend and relief it is to get a little elbow-room, a little broad freehand work, a chance of action not absolutely determined letter and line by Codes and Manuals. The Civilian is not abusing Codes and Manuals; he knows they must exist; but oh, the relief of getting away from niggling and pottering over Section X Subsection Z to a wider world where one lays out roads and reservoirs, plans forest reserves and areas for cultivation, settles questions of rights and tenures, has, in a word, a chance of getting something done that shows. But the Civilian must not enlarge too much upon these lines, for he has to remember that you, his masters, will never be called upon to work either in the Agency or in the Plains or to look inside either a Code or a Manual, and that of all bores upon a bore-encumbered earth another man's shop is the worst.

When it comes to camping in the Agency you are reduced to the elementary means of locomotion altogether. The whole place being heaved up above the level of the normal earth and no one on the normal earth desiring it nearer, there are nothing but the merest tracks between it and the lower country; there is a ghat road here and there, but so few and far between that it is highly improbable that they will be any great use to you. There are therefore few means by which a cart can be taken to the Agency, and there are naturally few cart-roads on the top in consequence. Some of the paths are practicable for a horse and most are not; and horse food being bulky to carry and the syce only another creature to give trouble, the wise man leaves his steed below. One falls back therefore on the services of my lord the elephant, on manual labour and on one's own legs. Now there are elephants and elephants, and to those who know there is as much difference between the paces of the regal beasts designed and trained to carry a prince's howdah and the lumbering hitching baggage-animals as there is between a racer and a cab-horse. The elephants which the Government supply to such as the Civilian are not meant for passenger work; you *can* ride them, but it will tire you almost as much as if you had walked. Moreover, an elephant is an expensive thing both in original cost and in maintenance and they are consequently scarce, and after one or two experiences of the Agency coolie in carrying your baggage and falling down inebriate by the wayside, you will thereafter employ your elephant just as much as you can. You are left therefore to that method of getting forward for which nature has designed you—and you walk. If there is a very long march or a very steep bit in the middle—and Agency marches can be both long and steep—you may get a wooden office chair and lash two bamboos one on either side of it and so be carried on the shoulders of men. But this has its drawbacks; you will have to descend into ravines and gullies by outward-tilted paths a foot or so in width, and if the chair lists over—which it is always very liable to do—you are caught in a trap, for no power on earth can get you out of it in time and down you must go with the ship and all hands. The extraordinary sort of closed box in which the Aryan brother delights to be carried to his weddings or buryings or to any *tamasha* which happens to be toward is, needless to say, worse than the chair. The Civilian once tried an ordinary Ashantee hammock, but that was a total failure because you cannot sit up in a hammock and you cannot lie down in a topi. (Now of all the curses which beset unhappy souls in India, not excepting snakes, counterfeit coin, prickly heat and bandy-drivers, the topi is indeed the worst; and though you have the fortune to escape all others, this you must inevitably suffer.) But to walk long ways is very good and pleasant exercise, and it is so extraordinarily rare in India to find that walking is even endurable that one ought really to be very glad of the chance.

All the time one has to combat the arch enemy, the malaria, for he is the most subtle of all the fevers of the field and he will creep in in an instant just when you are off your guard. You must therefore never be off your guard. Our ancestors firmly believed that malaria was induced by drinking bad water, by sitting in a certain kind of mist, or by sleeping to windward of the fire; and your servants to this day suppose that it is acquired by eating oranges—in which belief they are of course to be encouraged for obvious reasons. But those who have studied and know do now affirm that malaria is a much more subtle devil than this and has hidden himself in the biting apparatus of the anopheles mosquito. It is just possible that you in the depths of your abysmal innocence believed that there was one beast called the mosquito and one only. Never was there a greater mistake. The Civilian has a friend who will reel you off at least seventy different kinds, and even he admits that he is only on the fringe of the subject and that he has made no special study of the *Culices.* This friend of the Civilian's would never dream of alluding to a mosquito. He would very likely ask you with a puzzled air what a mosquito was. He will exclaim to you, "Ah! Stephensi!" or "This is interesting; here we have the larvæ of Wilmori mixed up with those of Culicifacies." So you see that the enemy's forces are strong and by no means so simple as one would think; and if Stephensi or Wilmori or Culicifacies or any of their friends get at you, then it is perfectly certain that ten to fifteen days thereafter you will be unwell. So one has to avoid the haunts of these creatures and keep one's camp well away from villages and cover oneself up sufficiently and wear long boots in the evenings; and even then you go to sit up for a panther and Culicifacies arriving in force has you at his mercy. . . . But the Agency is worth a little malaria now and then, and unless you behave foolishly there is no special reason why it should ever become very bad.

The sad thing about the Agency is that it is a sort of gigantic Sweet Auburn; everywhere one comes upon lamentable manifestations that things were not always as they are now. Going through the dense jungle grass on a hillside you will suddenly drop a couple of feet or so over the stonework of a terraced wall; and looking round you will see that the growth of *yegisi* and *karraka* and the other odd Agency trees is young and thin, and that not so very long ago all this hillside which is now a sheet of jungle must have been carefully made and cultivated lands. You will come upon crumbling houses in the forest-glades deserted for months or even years, and others with the traces of the last cooking-fires of their owners still upon the stones. You will find streams trickling down the higher hills through spongy bog-land in which you can just trace filmy lines and squares that were at one time the boundaries of fields laboriously built into the hillside and sown and reaped more laboriously still. You will notice a little shola of trees left round the fountainhead of the spring, and among and around these you may work out traces of long-forgotten foundations, an ant-devoured fragment of wall, a casual stone set upon end to which some one once did worship.

Everywhere there is evidence of a vast depopulation, and in one or two places there are signs that the former people were something better than those of to-day. The temples of these present times, wherein are housed such gods and goddesses as still deign to preside, are the merest hovels of mud and thatch. Indeed, it is only in the exceptions that there are temples at all; generally a pointed stone stands up or a group of stones—five, very often, for the Five Pandava Brothers whose battle-car was driven by Krishna and who stand to the country peoples of South India as the Heroes did to Ancient Greece. But away in two very remote villages, hidden behind enormous and formidable hills, the Civilian has found temples of the finer sort, mouldering in ruin now but built originally with all the lavish decoration and all the cunning of design that the most notable workmen could apply. These were not built by such as inhabit these places now; but the total indifference of the Indian to historical relics has closed a door alike upon their past and upon their builders. "It was done in the time of our ancestors," is all you are ever likely to get—if, indeed, you get so much.

Once—in the Plains this was—the Civilian was walking across some very dull paddy-fields in a very commonplace and wearisome piece of country, and he came suddenly upon a mound from the top of which a black stone bull of Shiva sat gazing at him on a brick plinth. It occurred to the Civilian that here was something interesting and unusual and he made inquiry of his retinue and of the local people who were round him. He asked what it was for, and they said it was not for anything; and he asked who put it there, and they looked at each other and grinned foolishly; and he asked them if they knew anything about it at all, and they said they did not. The only positive reply he received was made by the Revenue Inspector, and what he said, in the dreary and slightly condescending tone which Revenue Inspectors affect, was, "That represents a cow, your honour." The Civilian then saw clearly that their minds were differently constructed and thanked him courteously and passed on. But from the Fable of the Civilian and the Archæological Ryots, you may learn how futile it would have been to make any inquiries as to the dead temples in the Agency; and so you must pardon the Civilian if he can tell you nothing about them—for he knew much better than to ask.

Except when he is led astray upon the golden path of dacoity—which is rare except in one or two villages where the thing is a tradition—your Agency villager nowadays is as peaceful and harmless as his own goats; this again was not always so. At Narasapatam, a hot and rather dreary place set in the one dull spot of a delightful country and chosen naturally therefore for a headquarters, the walls of the Taluk Office compound are fortified to this day with heavy gates and battlemented bastions, one at each corner. This was done because of a former tendency of the gentle hillman to come out in wild aimless raids inspired mainly by excess of arrack and the pomps and vanities of a house of turbulent zamindars who have now ceased to exist save as prisoners of the State; and though it is not recorded that they ever got the length of Narasapatam, which is a good ten miles out into the Plains, still they did achieve some very violent deeds of fire and sword, and it was always as well to be prepared. They were scarcely rebellions, these outbreaks, though some of them are so called in history, but rather a letting off of steam and a working out of the fiery essences of the *mohwa* and the sago-palm. There is hardly a trace of them left. Once the Civilian on a very high hill came to a curious L-shaped wall four feet high or so and built after the manner of a Scotch dry-stone dyke;

and he was told that it was a hundred years old and was a fort in one of these *fituris* or outbreaks. In this hill were some very curious caves which might well have been used by the Forty Thieves themselves; one of them, into which the Civilian ventured, was only a mere pinhole in the face of the hill through which it was possible and no more to squeeze, but inside there was a fairly spacious chamber running back into the mountain. The Civilian would have been glad to know and to tell you the history of these places, for he thinks it was probably interesting; but like all the Agency they have no history. Heaven knows what men first trod out these immemorial paths and battled and traded over the face of the everlasting hills and who built the ancient temples and founded the earliest forts; and it is not a thing that any of us are ever likely to learn. Men say the Agency has a future and so it would need, for it has certainly no accessible past.

And so you know now all that the Civilian can tell you about the Agency, or at all events all that it would interest you to hear; and you may have formed some idea why it is that the men who come out from civilized and cultured English homes amaze their Indian friends by jostling and falling over one another in the struggle to get to these realms of tents and tigers and many discomforts. The Civilian could take you with him to the tops of these cold mountains, where the great winds would sweep and tear at you and the thin keen air would clear your minds like a refreshing sleep, and he thinks you would humbly ask to be allowed to stay. But all this about the Agency has been a digression—naturally enough, for it was a digression of the Creator when He made it and a merciful digression of the British Raj when it was deciding what parts of India it would take; but we have a way to follow and digressions must not be. Let us go back to decent society, to A.D.C.'s and Secretaries and English ladies, for the bell rings for the last lap and we must get us to the Hills.

VIII

THE ROOF OF THE WORLD

A GREAT many people when they talk about going to the Hills mean Simla. The Civilian has never been to Simla, and he is sorry for this, for he believes it to be a wonderful and coruscating place. But he has been to Ootacamund which some call the finest hill-station in all Hind; and he has wandered the length and breadth of the Nilgiris which he is quite sure are the finest hill-country anywhere. The Nilgiris are a very large triangular rock which comes on at the south end of the Mysore plateau and then falls away sheer into the plains of Malabar and Coimbatore. The sides of this rock are very steep, but the top of it is more or less flat, and upon this top those fortunates who have obtained leave, or those still more fortunates who do not require any leave at all, go to and fro about their diversions.

This top is the Roof of the World—there is room on it for several towns, a number of excellent roads, many forests and jungles, some tea and coffee estates, a brewery of beer and a very considerable stretch of rolling down country where one may hunt the jackal. You cannot hunt the jackal at

Simla and you cannot see the eternal snows at Ooty, so you must just take your choice. Up the steep sides of the Nilgiris the amazing invention of man has contrived a railway; there is also a road which persons of fashion and nerve possessing motor-cars appear to prefer, but the Civilian, having no motor-car at the time and never at any time a sufficiency of nerve, did not.

He went up therefore by the railway. He does not think it is a patch on the Ceylon one, but then it has not the same chance, being very much shorter and so preoccupied with its task of getting to the top somehow that it spends most of its time burrowing along through cuttings and tunnels. If you take your seat on the proper side of the carriage you will at one stage have very fine outlooks on the plain country; but on the other you will only see the bank with snakes sunning themselves thereon and many wonderful butterflies. On this side also, however, you will see a rock two thousand feet high with a waterfall coming down it. With this you may as well content yourself, for it is not much use in any case trying to get on the right side of the carriage, as you are sure to find that the missionaries have seized it long before you could get near. There are always missionaries on the Nilgiri Railway and they know all about it. The Civilian got into a carriage with a number of them and they depressed him by telling him that he would certainly be suffocated in the tunnels because the smoke of the engine all came backwards; they also told him he would suffer all the symptoms of approaching heart failure when he passed the five thousand foot level, and would probably die altogether on the top. The Civilian was alarmed and was just going to get out when the train started and he found the engine pushed from behind, so there was no smoke; he then knew that the missionaries belonged to the Cold Water School and feared no more, and even though they told him the most dreadful stories of accidents and landslips and so forth all the way up he was not disturbed and admired the scenery. Most of all he was consumed with envy of a railway man who sat on a little platform in front of the very front carriage of the train and was propelled upwards like a god, smoking cheroots and seeing all before him. The missionaries said the train would stick, but it didn't, but climbed up splendidly through a variety of stations with pleasant names, while the coco-nuts of the Plains gave way to the dense forest of the lower jungles and that in turn to the great stately timber of the higher hills; and gradually there set into the air that clear thin freshness of the high places which is quite different from the chill of the Plains after rain or the sharpest and most bracing wind that ever came in from the sea. And presently they drew up on to a level and came there to a foaming river and a town of the most extraordinary hideousness set amid every kind of beauty. This, it appeared, was Coonoor.

There are three towns on the Nilgiris—Coonoor which with the military hold of Wellington counts as one, Ootacamund, and, far away off the beaten track on the other side, Kotagiri. Ootacamund is the highest and Coonoor the lowest and Kotagiri the cheapest ; and the devotees of these three towns are as clearly demarcated one from the other as were the Mountain, Plain and Coast of Ancient Attica. If you live in Ootacamund you continually express your wonder that any one can be induced to live in so Bœotian a latitude as Coonoor ; and, on the other hand, if you choose to inhabit Coonoor you naturally give it out that of all places on earth you most despise and abominate Ooty. Coonoor calls Ooty stiff, and Ooty calls Coonoor vulgar—both in point of fact containing in the appointed places much the same amount of both qualities. Wellington is military and so out of the running, and of Kotagiri more anon.

The Civilian got out of the train at Coonoor, but at first it struck him as being rather hotter than the Plains, for he was having his first experience of the burning power of the hill sun which can remove your skin and turn you nearly black in two hours. This in the Plains the sun never attempts to do, which is a great mystery. The Civilian drove up an endlessly long terra-cotta hill through an involved and composite bazaar and was nearly scorched to death, and though he succeeded in the end in getting a very good lunch he thought he would not like Coonoor. He then turned his mind to Ooty, but on inquiry he found that there was nowhere in all Ooty where such as he could stay, as the nobility had bought up all the houses and the gentry were occupying all the hotels. But at the establishment where he had the good lunch they told him that there was a place called the *Blue Mountain Hotel* at Kotagiri; and being pleased with the name, which is always a great thing in spite of what poets have said to the contrary, the Civilian got into a two-horse vehicle and drove thirteen miles along a road of such turns and twists and hills and precipices that he was like to go grey in an afternoon. He was just beginning to think there could be no such place as Kotagiri and that he had been carried off by brigands, when sure enough they did come to the *Blue Mountain Hotel.* There was no blue mountain, however—though there were mountains of most other colours—nor even a painted signboard which there should certainly have been with a name like that. With the exception of this trifling defect, however, there was nothing wrong with the *Blue Mountain Hotel*; the Civilian abode there many days and he had nothing for it but praise.

There is only one subject on which the peoples of Coonoor and Ooty meet on common ground, and that is Kotagiri. Of all depressing, bourgeois, stale, flat and unprofitable places, they maintain, Kotagiri is the worst. It is entirely inhabited by the most tedious type of missionary, mostly of alien extraction; no one ever does anything; every one is socially impossible; there are no games, no amusements, nothing to do; it cannot be got at; it is ruinously expensive; and the food is bad. All this they said and to all this the Civilian listened politely, knowing that inasmuch as he had rashly admitted that he was going to Kotagiri this was the sort of thing they were bound to say; and when they had exhausted themselves he induced them to allow that the place possessed the seventh best climate in the world and commanded the finest shikar country in the Nilgiris. Being not inexperienced in the ways of the Cold Water School, this description rather cheered him than otherwise, and what followed was more or less what he had anticipated. He was disappointed in the climate which was hotter than he had been led to expect, and by the shikar which at that season was practically nil. In all other respects the place was most satisfactory and the indictments of the Civilian's informants proved to be a total misrepresentation of the facts. This, as he said, he had expected. For it is one of the strange features of life in India that if you ask a man about anything or anybody of which or of whom he is totally ignorant he will instantly reply without a moment's hesitation that it or he or she is awful, out of the question, impossible. This is really one of the symptoms of the Orientalization of the English in India, as the Civilian may one day show; for that is a great problem on which he fears he will yet have to speak.

In the meantime, however, let us eschew all problems and deal honestly with the Hills. Elsewhere and frequently the Civilian has mentioned that peculiar quality of Indian scenery—its resembling anything except what it is supposed to be; and this of course reaches its climax in the Hills.

Except where you have a tea plantation or tree-ferns, or where you come for a moment upon a glimpse of the great precipices and abysses about the edge of the rock, the place is almost indistinguishable from the lower highlands of Scotland. There is, of course, no heather, but then—contrary to reputation again—there is very little heather in that part of Scotland; but the real factor that creates the resemblance is the number of eucalyptus trees. This sounds strange, for eucalyptus trees are not common in Scotland, but Scotch firs are, and the effect of these two trees in a landscape is more or less identical. How this comes about the Civilian could never exactly ascertain, for the eucalyptus trees, when you come near them, are the most odd-looking things and have no resemblance to Scotch firs or anything else; it must be something in the bareness of the lower part of the trunk and the way the thin pointed foliage is put on in tufts and bunches. At all events there it remains; there is a golf course at Kotagiri which so far as appearances go might well be at Lothianburn or Stirling. Dodabetta, which is the top point of the Nilgiris and gets well on towards nine thousand feet, presents itself to you when you are near it as a roundish green hog's-back with a crescent of fir-wood running up one side; it might easily belong to the Pentlands or the Ochils except that it does not look quite sufficiently exciting. The road from Coonoor to Ooty runs up a broadish valley marked out in steadings and villages and patches of cultivation that might almost be Cromdale. One end of Ooty is exactly like Dunkeld or the Pass of Killiecrankie—towering hills of forest and rock; the other, where the hunting is done, is like the Braids, or the Downs of the English coast. The very houses are bungalows in the sense known to the London house agent; and the villages and farms are built into terraces in the hillsides with the air of Scottish crofts. But for a certain newness about the road-work and the buildings you might be almost anywhere between Leeds and Pitlochry. Yet the fact remains that you are only a little more than ten degrees from the Equator, and very considerably south of the Sahara Desert and the Red Sea.

You can get rid of this impression, however, very easily by simply taking yourself to the edge of the rock and poising on the topmost of that great sweep of scarps and precipices that falls down into the steaming feverish jungles and the damp coco-nut topes of the plains below. These are wonderful slopes, for they are clad in jungle wherein anything may dwell, jungle so thick that the sun's rays can hardly pierce it, and they are so steep that one feels quite ready to fall over and drop five thousand feet into one of the little townships one sees beneath. The Civilian always found it most startling to catch a glimpse of the plains; otherwise one always conceived oneself as walking about in low country with hills around one and forgot that the whole place was lifted up to begin with to immense altitudes. The plains lie out before one like a sea and there is no limit to the distance you can look out over them; they appear quite golden in colour with touches of red and merge finally into a golden-grey haze. You are above the clouds and see them passing on their ways; you are infinitely above all sounds—even the village drums—and yet the whole thing looks as though you could toss a stone on to any given spot with ease. Round you stand up the vast ramparts of the hills, dropping in steps and terraces to fearsome depths, and far below, with wisps of cloud round its summit, you see the top of a hill that looked from the plains as if it touched the heavens. It is quite wrong to say things look like a map, for a map is a flat plane on which you look down, whereas here you look out so far that the plains rise up before you and have much more the effect of a coloured curtain hung before your eyes. It is nothing so lifeless as a map; it is, indeed, a magic curtain, for into it are woven all the threads of all the lives in India.

Once the Civilian, questing further afield, betook himself to a place called Kodanaad on the other side of the hills, and there he really did attain to the Roof of the World, all made of rock, with a second roof of golden cloud standing above it. He went to the verge of this and looked down into a wonderful place called the Mysore Ditch, which was obviously inaccessible to mortals and given over to the peoples of the wilderness; and on the other side of this he saw the Mysore plateau laid out like one of those fascinating models one comes upon sometimes in museums. On his right, through the mouth of this Mysore Ditch, he saw again the Golden Plains and to the left he looked along the sheer face of the hills. The Civilian lived there in a small tent in the embrace of a shola—that is, a little wood, a covert—and every morning he went out before it was light pursued by a cold and remorseless wind and mist, and saw the droves of sambhur hinds going down with the first daylight from the grazing grounds. He saw everything covered in a cloud with the tops of the hills standing up like islands; and presently the sun rose and that there is no describing at all. The Civilian crawled about on the tops of precipices for fifteen hours a day and sat for long intervals in crannies of the rock lest the wind should carry him away altogether. Ostensibly he was trying to shoot a big sambhur stag, but in reality he was doing nothing; and perhaps if he had paid more attention to the work in hand he might now have had a noble head to show for it, but as things are he is not sorry that he preferred to sit and gaze at the immensities about him. There are plenty of sambhur stags or at least plenty of places where you may go out and try to shoot them; but it is not every day one finds oneself on the Roof of the World and one must take good note of what one sees there.

When he felt too cold—which was not often, because this was in May and the Indian sun in May is something to reckon with anywhere—the Civilian descended a little into the warmer valleys on the face of the hills. There were great dark forests and unseen roarings of water and mighty falls and all round one the choruses of cicalas sang endlessly, following like soldiers their leaders' words of command. The Civilian was a little alarmed by these dark forests which he was told were full of all manner of dangers, but he did not meet with any very fearful experiences. The worst of these expeditions—which were otherwise very charming—was that one went on and on downwards without thinking, being led on like enchanted princes in the stories from one temptation to another, when, suddenly coming to an opening in the woods, one looked round and was dismayed to see one's home perched in the clouds inaccessibly above. The Civilian was constantly getting benighted in these places, and regards it as a special dispensation that he was not bitten by a snake or chased by a bear; both were certainly to hand. He would then fight his way home, with the help of the round moon and occasional distant lightning, through a terrifying land of living and misshapen shadows that made sport of him on all sides, and was very thankful when he came to the lights of a hill village or the comparative loneliness of a main road. The moonlight on the hills is not like that of the plains and one does not see very far by it, but though one does not see the abyss one knows it is there and the effect is as if one walked upon a fragment of land sailing somewhere in the air. It is just, in fact, what we should experience every day of our lives if we could feel that the world was a round ball in space instead of only knowing it. Contrary to what has often been supposed, it is not in the least an unpleasant feeling.

The Civilian never met any one on his wanderings; and this was perfectly natural, for he was behaving in an absurd and outrageous manner. It is not correct or even sane to go gaping at views or clambering about waterfalls or capering like a maniac upon hilltops in the dawn; what one should do—having paid handsomely to reach these places of noble prospect, of clear and perfect air, and having reached them after not inconsiderable travail to oneself—is to go to the Ladies' Annexe at the Club and there, surveying a stucco wall, enter closely into the affairs of A, B, C, X, Y and Z, knowing quite well all the time that these personages are doing the same for you. This is what bright novelists call the easy-going *camaraderie* of an Indian station. Now there is nothing that so delights the heart of the Civilian as to sit with a friend and revile some mutual acquaintance, and he is well aware that there is nothing like a mutual *bête noire* for making friends, but when one has sat in a circle at the Club and heard nothing but abuse poured out on every name known or unknown, dead or alive, that chances to come up for notice, one surely cannot rise with any other hope than that as soon as one's back is turned one's own name will be the next. A and B and C and the rest of them, however, do not seem to think of this and go on trusting with a childish and beautiful simplicity what they are pleased to call their set. The Civilian is privileged to know because he is a silent man and esteemed harmless and he has sat in A's set when A had gone and in B's while B played tennis a little way off, and saying little has heard much. He will be the first to admit that in these matters he is not quite right in the head and that his outlook is improper; but it does seem to him that if A has called on B and B has not called on C and X is keeping himself to himself and Y is keeping himself to Z, that is all very nice no doubt, but not any reason why we, our opinions not being asked, should excite ourselves so desperately about it. This is an old story and none of the Civilian's business after all; but on the Roof of the World it does seem rather a waste to be always grubbing and boring in its basement. He will say no more, for nobody will pay any attention to him; and after all it is doubtless a great diversion to that Personal Devil in whom he implicitly believes.

The inhabitants of the Roof of the World vary according to locality. On the side of Ootacamund and Coonoor they consist of aborigines and Brass Hats—this last being, for some inscrutable reason, the name bestowed by their compeers on the leading lights of Madras society. On the side on which the Civilian spent most of his time, they are aborigines and missionaries. An exiguous community of planters is scattered over all. Your planter is a grand fellow; and well he might be, for he lives in most delightful places, eats, drinks and smokes what he pleases, and is still allowed to speak of Indians as "natives." He lives now as—alas!—we all lived once, before we had to deal with the bogies of a reformed India and post-war prices; and it is even whispered that the day is approaching when he too must succumb. Setting aside the planter, then, because the Civilian envies him far too much to describe him, there is no doubt that the next most interesting of the hill-peoples are the aborigines. They do not obtrude themselves, and indeed A, B, C and company do not recognize them as existing or, at the most, express their annoyance that such emaciated and evil-looking objects should be allowed to encumber that ground which has been set apart for their enjoyment and holiday. On this point the aborigines have their own ideas and the Civilian would dearly like to hear what they really think of Messrs. A and B and C, but they do not tell.

There is a kind of them called Todas who are the very absolute aboriginal, wear only a blanket, keep savage buffaloes and do nothing from morn till dewy eve but sit about and look like the people one sees in elementary Bible picture-books or in cheap continental prints of the Twelve Apastles. Having seen a Toda, the Civilian now knows exactly what Esau was like, and can understand how it was that the aspect of him which most impressed the chronicler was his extreme hairiness. The Civilian has been told that the Todas are one of the most interesting peoples upon earth and that their manners and customs are illustrative of a great many prehistoric and critical things and that they are even, perhaps, the Genuine Dravidians; he quite believes all this, but will not enter upon the matter here because it has been done admirably elsewhere by those who really know. There are other aborigines called Kotas, and the Civilian used to meet droves of them wandering about the roads playing upon curious eight-foot horns and great humming drums—for they are a very musical people; there are also Badagas, but they are comparatively civilized. The Civilian has gone out shooting with a Badaga and he has seen the age-old cone-shaped Toda temples and been charged by a Toda buffalo on a narrow road, but his acquaintance with these races has not advanced much beyond this.

Now the Missionaries. Popular and heathenish belief has it that every hot weather without exception every missionary comes to the Hills for two months—an arrangement which strikes the Civilian as perfectly admirable. He thinks, however, that this can hardly be correct and that surely one or two must be left below, though there are certainly swarms upon the Hills. Missionaries are a terribly Controversial Topic and the Civilian must avoid them, but he thinks he must narrate the Fable of the Missionary and the Overworked Banker, which is one to remember, as are all moments in which our fellows give themselves away. The Banker's bank was an appallingly heavy one and he used to sit in it working from eight of the morning till seven or eight of the night; at this he did not cavil or complain, but bore it as well as he might. One morning as he sat in his veranda—and it was now towards the end of April—there came to call upon him a missionary to take his leave for the Hills. They talked for some little time and then the missionary said that the real tragedy of one's life in India and what he felt the most was that it was impossible to remain with one's work all the year round. The Banker looked at the calendar and he saw from it that he had had no leave for four years; and he looked at the thermometer and from it he saw that if the temperature did not rise above a hundred and fifteen within the next six weeks he would be a lucky man; and with a great and honourable effort he told the missionary he was sorry for him and bade him good-day. But that day is remembered by the shroffs and the accountants and the peons and all the subordinates of the Banker as a day very far from good, for he raged like a roaring lion until evening. The Civilian suspects himself of being uncharitable, and he wishes to state here that he has met missionaries who spared themselves in nothing—one he used to encounter frequently in wild places who said to him always, "Have you seen my kit anywhere?" because in his good works he had taken no heed of it and it was lost; and for that man the Civilian had a respect he has withheld from Members of Council. But—there are others. In any case the Civilian must not dally over the subject of Missionaries; he must rein back and talk pleasantly about his birds and beasts.

He finds, however, that he was forgetting the Brass Hats. He has not much to say about them except that they have contrived to make Ootacamund more like Madras-in-the-Hills than could reasonably have been supposed possible. He does not think they take much interest in the Hills any more than anybody else: at any rate he never met any of them on his wanderings, and what they do with their time he has not the slightest idea. You may encounter their motor drivers taking their cars out for exercise on the road between Ooty and Coonoor, and unless you are a man of iron nerve it were better for you that you should walk in the jungle among nests of cobras and the honeycombs of wild and stinging bees than to take your exercise along a hill road of sharp curves whereon native drivers ply their masters' cars. The younger generation in India loves driving motors: its idea of a perfect run is to drive at thirty miles an hour along a twisting bazaar full of traffic with an electric horn and a foot-siren going the whole time. At night when a dazzling blaze of electricity can be added it is even better, and if a friend be at one's side to rend the air with shrill yelps, and execrate perfectly unoffending passers-by, then best of all. (How much more agreeable than a great rough ill-mannered brute of a horse such as the mad European is wont to maintain, which is no use to his servants whatever.) How grand to scatter the passers-by this way and that; to terrify the cart-bullocks so that the whole thing with its load of women and little children goes hurtling into the ditch; to speed up with shouts and blastings for the edification of some old coolie woman; with all the time the delightful knowledge that if one smashes the car to bits no compensation that one's master can recover from one is likely to be of any use to him. It is a pleasant form of service, moreover, commanding good wages for doing nothing, and offering many opportunities for profitable and almost undetectable larcenies in the lines of petrol and oil. Yes, indeed, your smart native driver can take your pleasure from your car quickly enough and cause you to loathe the day you bought it. . . . But we seem to have wandered away from the Brass Hats; perhaps after all that is the best and safest thing we can do.

The tragedy of going to the Hills is the tragedy of soaring everywhere—you have to come down again. And when you have descended that wonderful railway for about three-quarters of its length you will come to a place called Kullar or some such name, and there you will get out to walk upon the platform, and suddenly with all the vigour of a love long and purposely lost the heat of the Plains will throw its arms around you and claim you once more for its own. That is an awful moment, and it is a moment that is apt to lengthen itself into days before you begin to give up wondering whether it is not worth while to retire from your service and invest all your savings in one wild effort to become a planter. The Civilian is clearly convinced in his own mind that the only reason every one does not put this into force is that after coming down from the Hills they *have* no savings.

But you, good masters, existing as you do only in fancy, have no call to descend and the Civilian has no intention in the meantime of descending with you. See now—he has brought you and disembarked you on the Edge of India and he has conducted you through the countries of the Plains and he has lodged you upon the Roof of the World. There is no earthly sense in going further. But before our ways part we shall have up a stirrup-cup and over it we shall foregather for a space, for the Civilian is selfish and has still one or two things which he wishes you to hear. Let us sit down therefore on the cold hill-tops among the Todas and the sambhur deer, and while you look out over the Golden Plains—fairy gold, no doubt, but let us forget that for the moment—the Civilian will talk yet a little longer, wisely and altogether at large.

PART II

PEOPLE

IX

INDIGENOUS

NOT very long ago the Civilian was going up to a house upon a hill and all his luggage was being carried before him. Ten coolies were carrying it, and of these nine ran on speedily and well. The tenth lagged. But the Civilian, knowing that the bundle this man carried was vital to his evening's enjoyment—contained the cartridges or some such indispensable—kept close upon his heels prodding him on with a stick. The nine good coolies vanished from sight, but still the tenth lagged, going just as slowly as man could crawl and just two feet ahead of the Civilian. He was not tired, he was not weak, he was not lame or drunk or in any way incapacitated; he had simply made up his mind that he was going to do the thing in a certain time, in just that time, in no less and in no more.

The Civilian thought that if he kept close at his heels with the noises of one stepping out briskly the coolie would go on; but he didn't. He wanted the Civilian to pass him so that he might sit down at the roadside and be at peace, and this the Civilian —for reasons above stated—was determined not to do. Every five yards the coolie came to an almost dead stop and had to be prodded; he crawled on another five yards, slacked off and was prodded again. It was four miles to their destination, and the coolie won a good mile and a half from home. He would have gone on with the stopping and prodding process right up to the bungalow door, once every five yards as regular as clockwork; the Civilian couldn't. There came a point where his nerves gave way and he had to pass the coolie and go on. His walk was utterly spoiled. The coolie came in an hour and a half late and the Civilian's evening was utterly spoiled also. It is true that he did not pay the coolie, but by that he saved only four annas, and four annas is a poor recompense for an evening wrecked.

That is one story; here is another.

Once upon a time the Civilian and a friend arranged to go to a certain place and shoot bears. To shoot these bears one went out through the stubble-crop by moonlight with hunting dogs and with persons of the Kshatrya caste armed with spears. These things were necessary because without local knowledge one was lost. Now the Civilian and his friend were twain, and if twain go to the shooting of one bear there is nothing to expect but trouble. Therefore the Civilian and his friend propounded to the Kshatrya people that they should go in two parties, each taking one dog. The Kshatryas said they should all go together; the Civilian and his friend said they would not; the Kshatryas agreed and went away. Came the hour of the sally and behold there was only one dog and the Kshatrya who was to lead the second party was sick. They went forth after some recrimination, and presently the Civilian had a hallucination that a second dog had joined them and that the sick Kshatrya was coming along in the rear. Soon he became persuaded that it was even so. Presently appeared a bear and the Civilian and his friend, loosing off together, filled the night air with hideous wrangling. Again the evening was a dismal failure. But the Kshatrya people had had their way.

You have now heard the Fable of the Lagging Coolie and the Fable of the Implacable Kshatryas. The moral of these two tales is to be found in the verses of a certain libretto cited by Mr. Kipling but not otherwise generally known :

It is not good for the Christian's health to hustle the Aryan brown,
For the Christian riles, and the Aryan smiles, and he weareth the Christian down ;
And the end of the fight is a tombstone white with the name of the late deceased
And the epitaph drear : " A fool lies here, who tried to hustle the East."

" He weareth the Christian down." By Heaven ! but he does. The Civilian will pray for you that you may never be set to wrestle with the frightful patience, the awful ability to wait for ever, the grim gift of going on and on and taking no notice, that dwells in the deeps of the Indian soul. It is a thing that makes light of centuries and it will come and come and come again for ever. It will spend itself upon a trifle as freely as upon a kingdom. It is not a thing for human beings to fight against and people who fight long against it cease rapidly to be human beings. It is all very well for such people to call themselves the Dominant Race and so on, but as a matter of fact they either become Orientalized or else, as Mr. Kipling says, they simply die. It is very largely a matter of choice. Now the Orientalization of the English in India is a wonderful and interesting thing and in due time the Civilian may find occasion to say something thereanent.

In the meantime, however, consider the Fable of the Sweeper's Cow. Once upon a time Mrs. Civilian, coming to a new station, desired a cow to be brought to her bungalow so that she might personally see it milked and thus obtain some milk which, if thin and poor, would at least be unadulterated. Now this is a thing which rends the lower-class Indian's soul. He would rather face a hundred Gehennas than supply a bag of paddy without a measure of sand, rather than sell you sugar unmixed with chalk, a thousand times rather than sell you a can of milk which did not contain a percentage of dirty water. Therefore, amiable fellow, he refused to send his cow to Mrs. Civilian's bungalow. Now Mrs. Civilian was at this juncture informed that the lady who condescended to sweep out the bungalow for a consideration of seven rupees a month possessed a tolerable cow and, being able to bring pressure to bear in this quarter, had this cow brought. But that night the family of the sweeper assaulted the informant of Mrs. Civilian because the informant had given it away that they had a cow, that they were rich people and thus as an inevitable result the pay of the sweeper would be reduced. Now the sweeper was paid at the rate of seven rupees a month because that appeared a reasonable return for the work she did, but this was not at all how the matter appeared to the sweeper—nor how it would have appeared to any other Indian of the same class. An office peon, for instance, regards the thing from exactly the same point of view. You pay the dependent in question because he is poor and you charitable, because he has a large family and you have a large income, because it is *mamul* for him to be there and for you to pay him, because it is more blessed to give than to receive—because of anything and everything on earth you like except because he has done a job of work and has thereby earned a proportionate wage. The acceptance of a situation in India entails no obligation to carry out its duties: it simply means that you have obtained some one's "favour" and are henceforth provided for. Europeans pay certain sums to certain people because Europeans are mad or because God has willed it so; that is all there is to it. Imagine an English carpenter, having done his job, sending in his bill and cadging for a shilling tip; yet that is what every Indian carpenter—having first presented you with a series of perfectly imbecile estimates—will assuredly do. In this part of the world nothing has any price; it is *Taima chittam*—your Honour's pleasure, or what one can screw out of the nearest fool. Your peon realizes that by the grace of God he draws so much a month; but ask him to set his hand to a turn of work and he will stare and gape. This is a fundamental; but the Civilian thinks that after two hundred years of British administration it is a depressing misunderstanding to encounter.

It is also a little tedious, when wrestling with such difficulties, to be regarded calmly as the afflicted of God, as a creature who has come to India for enlightenment and is obtaining it but slowly, as a poor imbecile, scarcely deserving more than a pitying smile. We come here to the Great Irreconcilable—the intense distrust of the European, and the perfectly amazing credulity, the stupendous gullibility, of one Indian towards another. The Civilian might betake him to a village—to any village you please to name—and might there expound the Savings Bank or Money Order System or the War Loan or any other sound and business-like affair, and he would elicit nothing but head-shakings and murmurs of dubiety; but at his heels there might come a smart gentleman in a *dhoty* and a linen coat giving himself out as the collector of subscriptions for the building of a temple in Pondicherry or a pleasure-garden in Timbuctoo, and that man would depart with his pocket full of rupees. The Civilian had a motor once and a motor-boy; and though the Civilian drove about before their eyes it was considered that he knew nothing but what the motor-boy told him, while the motor-boy, who, incidentally, could not take in a word that was said to him by any one whatsoever in any known language, was regarded as the last word in mechanical genius. The Civilian does not say that this is a very serious matter, except that it places such a card in the hand of the Oriental scoundrel (who is legion) as against the Oriental dupe (who is omnipresent) and as against such as the Civilian (who might otherwise intervene), but he is prepared to maintain that it is exceedingly irritating. Remember that the climate of India is hot and that one suffers from mosquitoes and prickly heat.

The Civilian will also admit that he is petty enough to be vexed by the immensity of Oriental conceit. Let us admit that beside the Hindu philosophers, Immanuel Kant was a babbling babe, that Tagore outshines Shakespeare as the sun the stars, and that in music, dancing, sculpture, architecture, painting and everything else, all is in proportion. Let these things be *ex hypothesi.* Let one admit one is a junior and all unversed in the mysteries of Hind. It is still a trifle trying to be told by one's dressing-boy, who the other day was scrubbing the pots outside someone's kitchen, that the suit one brought out from home is badly cut and that one is choosing the wrong tie. It is still a shade wearisome to be informed by one's peon (who was formerly a washerman) that one has pitched one's tent in the wrong place and has brought the wrong kind of cartridges for shooting snipe. It is the least thing in the world galling to be patronized by the fifth clerk of one's office on questions of general principle. It is in some degree exasperating to learn that a pleader whose speech is a congeries of ill-assimilated catchwords and whose accent rends the suffering ear like a locomotive whistle, knows English better than you do, writes it better than you can, and speaks it far, far better than you ever will. Yet all these things have happened to the Civilian and to others like him, and they would happen to you, good sir, if you were here to-day. The Civilian is aware that these are minor afflictions and merely laughable, and nine times out of ten he will laugh at them with you very heartily. The tenth—such is the frailty of human intellect and such the cursedness of life in India—they will throw him—and you—into a passion of which we will not get the better for several days.

And lastly in this category—and this is the worst of all and a very serious thing indeed, and as, in a sense, it proceeds from them, it makes the other items serious as well—there is the gruesome fact that after enduring all these and more, after two hundred years of trying to understand and sympathize, after thousands of our best have laboured their fill and gone their ways, after all this we remain on the very verge. The Magistrate who tries a case will be, at the end of the proceedings, the man who knows least of the truth. The Divisional Officer who inquires into a land or water-rate dispute will never know even so well as the veriest pariah of the village what really underlay the matter. The best Collector that ever was might possibly know the most of what was being said in his District, but he could never know the one-tenth part of what was being thought. You may open your heart to all comers. you may be accessible day and night, you may bait your confidence with kindness and sympathy, but your butler will always know more about your dearest project than you will and your duffadar, your head-peon, will know twice as much again. And they will be as graven images. It is a terrible thing to have power and no data, to have to decide and rule without evidence, to struggle constantly with the black devil of suspicion, to delve night and day for the ulterior motive. Yet that is how the most of us stand, and if you set out to fish for truth, she has lain so long at the bottom of the well of Lies that she will come to you drowned in them and unrecognizable. If you doubt this, you have only to obtain one single honest servant. This is a Herculean task, but it can be done, for the Civilian once had one—a Eurasian—and his eyes were opened. He will pray for you that if you come to India such a one may never be yours, for on the whole it is worse than the other thing.

Then what in the name of all that is wonderful are we doing in India at all? What, indeed. The Civilian cannot tell you, for he does not know, but he does think we are doing something. He thinks this because of a letter he saw the other day in the papers. It was a letter signed by a number of Indian gentlemen, and they asked that their District which had had an Indian Collector for some years past might be given a European Collector for a change. Now, if there is anything in Self-Government for India at all, an Indian Collector ought to be its finest product, and the raising of Indians to be Collectors should be India's noblest aim. The Civilian is, moreover, competent to state that the Indian Collector in question was a first-class man and an able. But they wanted a European. There you are, and the Civilian leaves you to make of it what you can. He himself, frankly, is beaten.

What, then, about Self-Government for India? If the Civilian were a Member of Council writing a deep and instructive work he would allow himself to be drawn into a discussion of this interesting problem; as it is, being merely the Civilian and having no licence—or desire—to instruct, he means to let it go. He does not know very much about it and you have given him some reason to suppose that your interest in it is but slight. Moreover, he holds the absurd and revolutionary idea that India is self-governed already. It is governed by Head Clerks and Huzur Sheristadars and all the legion of people who put up inviting little Office Notes for Your Honour's signature. Now "signing at the place marked" is assuredly a shameful way of getting through one's official papers, and the Civilian begs to assure you that he employs it not, nor do his fellows; but there are more ways of marking a place than by a cross in red on the file. The Civilian contends that the place is very often marked, and if India can mark the place then India is self-governed. He will obtain no support for this view which, with so many earnest-minded and diligent people about, is palpably frivolous and preposterous, but—he does not see what India has got to agitate about. As for Self-Government in its broader and more discussed aspect, he does not see any difficulty in finding Indian gentlemen to take on and ably fulfil the highest posts; the trouble will come in with the immense number of subordinate posts which Indian gentlemen will have to fill. The Civilian invites here a study of those petty authorities which are at present wielded by natives of India—station-masters, Sub-overseers in charge of irrigation works, Revenue Inspectors, Salt Inspectors, Police Inspectors, toll-keepers, Forest Guards. That is all he has to say about Self-Government for India.

While we are on the greater themes of life let us say our say also on Indian education. Others, who know, have said so much on this subject that little latitude is left for such a tyro as the Civilian even to make a fool of himself. He will confine himself, therefore, to recounting a single incident. Once, while the Civilian was wandering in that Agency which he has elsewhere attempted to describe, he came upon a school which he resolved to inspect. The pupils of this school could just read, they could just do very simple addition sums, they could scrawl a few pot-hooks on a slate; but one expected nothing more because they were really savages. It was suddenly announced, however, that there was a pupil who was advanced in geography. The Civilian greatly desired to see this phenomenon and a lumpish youth was promptly led to where there hung upon the wall one of those horrid unlettered "physical" maps that might be anywhere. It represented, as a matter of fact, a slice of the east coast of India. "Now show," said the teacher, "the District of N"—which was their district. The pupil described a rough circle on the map embracing a good deal of sea.

"Now point M"—which was the headquarters of this District. The pupil made a peck at the map as if he were killing a fly. "Dear me," said the Civilian, "this is really excellent. Now, sir, could you tell me how far it is from here to M?" He couldn't. "Can you tell me what direction you would go to it?" He couldn't. "Could you tell me how to get to X?"—X being the nearest market-town on the plains below. He couldn't. "Could you make me a little plan showing the relative positions of your village and its two neighbours?" Gape. "Do you know what a map or a plan is?" Blank. "Well, then, show me N on that map." He did it like a shot—as he could have done it a hundred and fifty times. You made a certain motion with your hand and that for some reason—God knew what—was N; you jabbed at a point and similarly that was M. Having done this you knew geography. Well?'

The Fable of the Civilian and the Geographical Expert is related because the Civilian wishes to say that it seems to him typical of a great deal of Indian education. There is something wrong about education in India, but whether it is the system or the teachers or the pupils or just the Personal Devil again the Civilian cannot for the life of him make out. He admits—remember that his connection with educational matters extends only to an occasional distribution of prizes—that the whole question of English education in India seems to him to be beset with appalling posers. How, for instance, are you to tackle fellows who are one age in body, another in soul, and quite another in mind? How are you to reconcile your British schoolboy, keen on games, essentially young, with your actual Brahmin youth who has been married for some years, is possibly a father, is aware of love both sacred and profane and is essentially mature ? Can you imagine Don Juan exciting himself over the batting averages of Surrey ? Can you conceive of Isaac of York spending a sleepless night over the result of the Senior Hundred Yards ? Can you picture to yourselves Alexander the Great, or any other who grew up too young, ragging in the Lower Third ? Who ever heard of a "Boy's Strike" at, say, the Bermondsey Board School ? Who ever heard of an "affray" in which the Sixth Form stabbed each other with daggers ? Who ever heard of a Fourth Form exam. in which the favourite was assassinated by poisoners suborned by the runner-up ? Who ever heard of a defeated school footer team endeavouring to bring a suit against the cup-winners because the ground on which the game was played was six inches too long ? Yet—take it from the Civilian, please—one has heard of these things in India. How then to apply the good old British methods of education ? The Civilian admits that he cannot tell you. You cannot, it seems to him, educate Indian boys on English lines, because by the time he has reached the school-going or educable age there is hardly such a thing as an Indian boy. If he hasn't started man's work on man's wages, he has started man's thinking on man's lines. He does not climb trees for nests or play at savages or pirates ; he writes eight-anna petitions for illiterates in the bazaar, and plays—with not so very much play in it—at being a vakil. And yet he has an eye for games that Chiron's pupils might have envied and an aptitude and sensibility that wise Centaur might well have prayed for in the sons of the Heroes. What, then, is one to do with him?

The Civilian has told you honestly that he doesn't know, and so we will speak no more of education. Instead he will now take his lance in his hand and set out to shatter the illusion of the Funny Native. Far too much has been written and read about the Funny Native; and though the Civilian is well aware that this will cost him in many quarters his reputation for a sense of humour he is going to say right out that it is so much tosh. At base, he thinks, it is just the good old attitude of John Bull on the Continent and so he lays much of it—though by no means all—at the door of the globe-trotter. The Indian servant, peon, coolie, artisan, tradesman, or lower-class subordinate is not really very funny, and the Civilian considers that the Globe-trotter aforesaid, the Passenger, and perhaps a few of the Six Months School are the only people who have ever found him so. (Of these personages more anon.) The Civilian will now wager and bet that one year's house-keeping—*pukka* house-keeping; no hotels; no Eurasian manageresses; no wastage—will cure any one of the illusion of the Funny Native. It may be funny for a month—or perhaps to really sunny natures for even six months—to live among a people whose aim and intention is to cheat you, to defraud you, to bewilder and bamboozle you, to exploit you for every anna, every half-anna, every pice and pie you are worth ; but at the end of that time the cream comes off the joke. " Surely one need not allow oneself to be so worried by mere servants ? " Come and try—in a hot country infested with stinging creatures. " Surely one should not take such people as one's representative type of Indian ? " Who said one did ? But remember your servants and subordinates and the trade and work-people about the bungalow form a large proportion of the Indians with whom you—or anybody else—are going to come into close contact, and for all practical purposes the *only* Indians your wife—or any one else's—is going to come in contact with at all. This is largely the fault of the better kinds of Indian ; but there it is.

Let us, then, observe some of the comedians at work. The Postal Peon throws your treasured home mail into the tank to save himself the trouble of delivering it ; the hospital compounder sends you round in an emergency adulterated trash ; the bazaar supplies you chalked sugar and watered milk. The carpenter after an extortionate overcharge puts up the punkah with rotten bazaar thread instead of with proper rope and down it comes upon you in the night and gives you a raging headache for your big case on the morrow ; a laughable incident. Your syce adulterates your horse's food with some filth from the bazaar and the horse dies in agonies ; most amusing. Your chokra gets drunk while you are in camp, takes out your new bicycle, rides it into a stone wall and smashes it in fragments ; funny fellow. Your dressing-boy wears your shirt and gives you eczema—if nothing worse ; a diverting idea. Mrs.

A's ayah gives the baby a dose of opium to keep it quiet while she intrigues with the butler and the baby dies; a screaming farce. Mrs. B's butler takes the Club soda and sells it in the bazaar and brings back at a profit some foul local production made of unfiltered tank water, and Mrs. B dies of enteric; the very spirit and essence of comedy. The Funny Native indeed! But the Civilian is becoming bitter again, and bitter people only bore; so let us leave the Funny Native to the funny fools who delight in him and get away to something on which the Civilian feels less strongly.

The Civilian said some little time back that one must necessarily, at the best, halt upon the verge, and unless one could disguise oneself like Strickland—who, by the way, must have been a most intolerable person in real life—or descend to the level of Macintosh Jelaluddin, a depth to which few in the interests of pure science are ready to go, one is certain there to remain. It is the biggest disappointment of India. As a result the Civilian cannot, as he would, lead you into these dark alleyways off the bazaar that look so fascinating—and are probably so beastly—he cannot tell you what is moving in the mind of yonder sleek and shaven Brahmin squatting meditatively in the dust; he cannot tell you what topics are really vexing the hearts of the dwellers in the by-ways; he cannot outline to you the real causes which underlay the quarrel between the brothers Ramaswami and Kanniah. He can tell you that the sanitation in the alleyways is shocking bad; that the Brahmin belongs to the Vydiki sect and is probably meditating mischief; that the dwellers in the by-ways will certainly be talking about food, money and intrigue; and that Ramaswami and Kanniah have brought a criminal charge and counter-charge in the Sub-Magistrate's court: but beyond this he cannot go. If he asked he would obtain nothing but lies. It is maddening—but there it is. The missionary—if he be the right sort of missionary—may be able to take you a little further; he may, for instance, be able to tell you that Messrs. Ramaswami and Kanniah have given him a fairly truthful account of the whole affair from the beginning—an account which they would rather die than emit in a court of law. The right sort of missionary can be a great help, and the Civilian will be the first to assert it. But even he, good man and patient friend, penetrates scarcely at all: and for such as the Civilian, the task is doubly hard.

The Civilian being a Civilian, his intercourse with the Indigenous is naturally more or less of an official order; it is also of course several stages removed. He would give much if neither of these things were so, but, as you will see, so they inevitably are. Suppose the Civilian to be in charge of a Division; in that Division there would be, perhaps, three Taluks, each under a Tahsildar. In the headquarters of each Taluk there would be a Sub-Magistrate for criminal and a District Munsiff for civil cases. In each Taluk there would be three firkas, say, and in each firka a Revenue Inspector. In each firka there might be fifty villages and in each village there would be a munsiff and a karnam—a village head and an accountant. In every office—Taluk office, Sub-Magistrate's office, Divisional office—there would be a galaxy of clerks, accountants, peons and menials. That would more or less account for the purely Revenue side of the Division. But besides all these the place would be swarming with Police; there would be subordinates of the Forests, subordinates of the P.W.D., mobs of subordinates of the Salt and Education. There would be a Local Fund Staff—with Overseers, Sub-Overseers, Minor Irrigation Overseers, more clerks, more peons. There would be Local Fund Hospitals and Dispensaries with Assistant Surgeons, Sub-Assistant Surgeons, and compounders and midwives and vaccinators. And there would be other varied flotsam and jetsam—items from the Land Records Department, Survey parties, Estate officials under the Court of Wards, Agricultural people and possibly Marine.

The Civilian does not for an instant desire you to master this elaborate scheme—only to read it through roughly and try to arrive at the vast cumulative effect of underlings. Remember that all these are in cross-correspondence with one another, and you will see that unless one is to go demented altogether things must pass, to use the official formula, "through the proper channels." A ryot might walk into the Civilian's grandfather's bungalow and state his case and see the Civilian's grandfather spring upon his horse and go out to settle the matter then and there; but that could hardly happen to-day. The ryot would have to be shunted back to his proper Tahsildar—unless, of course, it was something quite out of the common—who would in turn hand him on to his appropriate Revenue Inspector, and so in time he would come back again to the Civilian. Now whether the method of the Civilian or that of his grandfather is the better the Civilian is not prepared to say. It is true on the one side that the native does not like going to hospitals and that he hates vaccination and that he is slow to see the value or use of drains or waterworks or schools or scientific agriculture, and that he *did* like to have his little trouble looked into at once by the fountain-head of justice in the person of the Civilian's grandfather without all these middlemen to delay and worry; but on the other hand—well, on the other hand, of course, you have all that beautiful and complicated organism outlined above. And, also of course, there is lucrative employment for a great number of educated and cultured gentlemen in explaining the rules and working of that organism to the type of person who brought his petition to the Civilian's grandfather, which type of person, by the way—and this is perhaps a consideration—has not altered one single iota, and doesn't intend.

"But, Civilian, you have just said that your Division would be full of subordinates. Even though they are not all by any means directly under you, many must be, and with all at any rate you must come into close connection. Do you not meet and learn about these?" Officially, yes; personally, no—or at least not without immense patience and a persevering cross-examination so rude and so tedious that one can hardly go through with it at all. Any one of your subordinates will gladly tell you the story of his official life ten times a day if you will only listen; the difficulty is to avoid it. Once the Civilian was motoring along a dry and dusty road when he came to a Taluk office, and it occurred to him that he might procure him a coco-nut to drink. He was stopping his car when a figure immaculately clad shot from an office doorway and made him a low salaam. "Sir," said the figure, "my name is Hanumantha Venkataswami. I am the head accountant of this office. I have twenty-one years' service. I served for three years as copyist in the Divisional Office at Buchchipet. I was then Second Clerk in the Taluk Board Office at Madalpur, from whence I was promoted to act on fifteen a month in the Taluk Office at Gopalapatnam. Mr. Fitzjones, the then Collector, was so pleased with my work that he made me Probationary Revenue Inspector, and later his honour was pleased to say——" But the Civilian snatched hurriedly at his gear lever and fled thirsty from the accursed spot. Compared with these the Ancient Mariner was nothing and Sinbad with his Old Man of the Sea was to be envied.

On another occasion it fell to the lot of the Civilian to walk five miles across paddy-fields in the sole company of a garrulous Tahsildar, and the Tahsildar (who was ripe for a pension) began at the very beginning and told the Story of his Life. He had got about the length of his promotion to Fourth Accountant in the Collector's office on rupees forty (acting), when the Civilian felt he could endure it no more. So he asked him if it was not a fact that he did not get on very well with the late Sub-Magistrate. (It would have been no use asking him about the present Sub-Magistrate for he would not have said a word about him.) For the rest of the walk the Civilian was comparatively diverted. It had been a shot in the dark, but it brought down a wonderful bag. Ages and ages ago in his early youth the Civilian was intrigued with a young lady who worked in a milliner's shop and that young lady in her artless prattle gave him to understand something of the bitter jealousies, the amazing hates and tempers, the stupendous pettinesses that prevailed in that establishment. One would not have thought that the little bonnet-maker and the Tahsildar had much in common, but they had. They could have talked together for hours. Till he had that walk with his Tahsildar the Civilian had thought that the life of the millinery workroom was unique; but the Tahsildar gave him an exact and beautiful parallel. The Tahsildar was the little milliner's assistant, and the milliner's shop was the Revenue Establishment List. The Civilian was quite sorry when the walk came to an end.

"But surely the Story of the Tahsildar's Life should have been interesting." Yes, it should have been, but it wasn't. If the Tahsildar had told the Story of his Life as it really happened; if he had told the struggles he had, the mistakes he made, the difficulties he met and overcame, his own private doings and strivings and what he thought of it all in the end—then the Civilian would have sat him down upon a paddy-bund and begged him to talk on till midnight. But you must remember that he was a Tahsildar. As a result his entire story was told to show how he had been the smartest copyist ever known, the most accurate and diligent clerk, the most upright and competent Revenue Inspector, the finest accountant, the ideal Sub-Magistrate; and, moreover, how So-and-so had been pleased to commend him for that and Such-and-such had recorded a minute of praise for this and Government had sent him their thanks for the other thing. The Civilian once met a wise man, and the wise man had an idea that a little book should be published to advise a native subordinate how best to impress his superiors—which of course must be his object—on the rare occasions on which he sees them. In that book the first rule was to be: "Remember that self-eulogy is distasteful to European ears." The Civilian does not know if the wise man ever published his book—he hopes he did—but if not, then he would be glad if some of his Indian friends would read these lines he has just written. They would do them good.

The rules in that book afford a speculation too fascinating to resist. The second rule, the Civilian thinks, would be: "Do not cringe. Do not, of course, for God's sake, patronize (which you are more ready to do than you yourselves would ever believe), but strike the happy mean. If you have anything to say or any request to make, come and say it and make it, respectfully, but like a man and not like a worm. Do not 'Beg to be permitted to humbly submit.' The Oriental can realize that a man holds him in no extravagant degree of respect, and can still take pleasure in seeing that man grovelling at his feet with nonsensical phrases; the European can't. You mean no harm by it any more than by your drum-banging and trumpet-blowing; they are both the customs of your country; but they both make the European feel a little sick—which is not, presumably, the result at which you are aiming." That would be the second rule.

The third rule, of course, would simply be: "In Heaven's name, try to cultivate a sense of humour."

And the fourth rule—but this it would be hardly worth while printing because no one would ever adopt it—would be: "Try your very hardest to believe that the man whom you see to have succeeded with your European superiors has succeeded because of merits of his own, and not because he has in some peculiar way obtained their 'favour.' 'Favour' as a means of exalting incompetence is a purely Oriental notion—at least we have to tell you so, and so far as you are concerned it *is*. Do not be always seeking and boring after an ulterior motive. If Indians had spent all the time on intelligent progress that they have spent in grubbing after ulterior motives we should all be happier and more useful men to-day. You do not believe—as my servants believe—that master's favour is to be gained by the administration of a dose of white powder in his curry; why then should you pin your faith to what is only a refined version of the same stupid bogy?" That would be Rule Four.

Now if you say that the Civilian has not given you a picture of his subordinates or of the more helpful type of progressive middle-class Indian, you have only to imagine a well-intentioned, diligent, domesticated man, intelligent in the extreme along certain lines, anxious to succeed, anxious to please, crossed by a devil of distrust but raised by an angel of industry—breaking all these four rules at once. And there you have him.

Well, then, if that is the sort of thing you are after you may get the Story of his Life from any official ten times a day as the Civilian has said; you may also, if you wish or if your duty demands it, gather in the scandal of the milliner's workshop. But, unless it is directly connected with some particular request that is to be made, you are unlikely to get anything more satisfactory. From time to time all sorts and conditions of men will come to call, but they will either have a request to make—in which case it will occupy their whole minds and they will be simply vacant on any other subject—or they will have come to "pay their respects," in which case they will want to sit and look at you and will not wish to discuss anything at all. The Civilian was very interested in caste-distinctions, in Indian astrology and in Indian music, and he tried all these subjects, but he never got any information. It is just conceivable that his visitors knew nothing about them; but in this connection hear now the Fable of the Collector and the Barmecide Conversation. There was once a Collector who rose one hot morning with a touch of liver and a vast accumulation of work before him, and he found—as was natural under such circumstances—that an official in whom he had no earthly interest was waiting to "pay his respects." Etiquette demanded that he must be seen, so the Collector told his peon to show the official in. The official came in and said "Good morning" and sat down. The Collector said "Good morning." They sat on opposite sides on the office table and looked at each other for five minutes by the Collector's watch and then the Collector said "You may take leave." The official took leave, and to this day nobody has ever suggested that he was in any way dissatisfied with his interview.

When he was writing about headquarters the Civilian said something about the Perpetual Interview and its terrors, but he did not then mention what is really a very sad thing—the appearance of the Incoherent Enthusiast. The Incoherent Enthusiast really has something to say: he wants to tell you all about Hindu Astrology or how to play the *vina* or about the purification ceremonies of Brahmins or pilgrimages or Ayurvedic Medicine or some other exceedingly interesting thing. And he talks and he talks and the words and sentences stream forth in marvellous succession, but there is not a single intelligible remark in them all—or if such a one appears to arise it is immediately contradicted by the next. That is, indeed, sad, for one is shy of telling him he is simply babbling at large and it would not make any difference to him if one did; and one has the mortifying knowledge that one is missing a great deal. The Civilian still hopes for the day when the card of the Coherent Enthusiast will be sent up; and it will be a day well-earned when it comes, for in hopes of the Coherent Enthusiast he has suffered many who have tried him hard.

That same wise man who devised the idea of the Book of Rules once said to the Civilian that the time when the ordinary ryot-class native of India was happiest, the only moment in his life, perhaps, when he was really happy at all, was when he walked into Court behind his pleader carrying that learned gentleman's books and papers. At the time the Civilian thought that this was an unjust remark, but some little experience of court work has convinced him that at any rate it covers a terrible truth. The fact remains that the passion for litigation in the heart of the Aryan brother, when once it really takes hold, is simply overpowering. A Policeman once divided Indians into two classes: those you couldn't induce to enter a court even as witnesses and those you couldn't by any means keep out of it; and the Civilian thinks the latter class must be the majority. What, for instance, would you understand by "criminal litigation"? Probably nothing; yet it is an accepted phrase here. It means something like this. Ramaswami desires to marry his daughter to Kanniah's son or to enter into partnership with Kanniah in steering a deal in gingelly or to get a loan out of Kanniah—in a word, to obtain some consideration from Kanniah. Kanniah is unwilling—won't hear of it. Ramaswami then sets out to annoy him by various petty—incredibly petty—devices. Kanniah is adamant. Nothing for it, then, but criminal litigation. Ramaswami files an elaborate complaint against Kanniah on the ground that Kanniah and some of his relatives waylaid the unoffending Ramaswami and voluntarily caused hurt to him and to his friends; to support this he smacks his grandmother over the head with a *lathi* and sends her off to get a Medical Certificate. Kanniah, getting wind of this, rushes in a counter-charge saying the whole assault and battery was the work of Ramaswami; in support of which he breaks the third finger of his maternal aunt and sends her flying for a Medical Certificate too. But in his heart Kanniah knows he is done. Ramaswami was first in the field and he has cornered the evidence securely; his Medical Certificate is ante-dated to Kanniah's; nothing for it but to give him best this time—and not forget. So Kanniah, we imagine, goes to Ramaswami and says "Curse you, take my daughter or my money or my gingelly or whatever it is you want." On the appointed day for hearing the case Messrs. Ramaswami and Kanniah appear and present a *rajinama*—a petition of compromise—saying they have made up and settled the business out of court. The Magistrate with a sigh of relief strikes off Calendar

Cases Numbers 427 and 428 and goes on to the next business. . . . Or again. Ramaswami and Kanniah are supporting with vigour a contest over a piece of land which began in the time of their grandfathers and has since been dragged through every original and appellate court that can possibly hold jurisdiction over it. Ramaswami's fertile brain thinks out a new method of getting at the question; meanwhile, to keep the thing open, he files a criminal complaint against Kanniah for trespass and assault. He engages for the case a pleader competent on civil law, leads all his suit witnesses and documents and traps the unwary and bewildered magistrate into making some pronouncement as to title in the course of his judgment. (No need for this, of course, but a native magistrate will fall into this sort of snare ten times out of ten.) Card number one to play for what it is worth in the new suit. Next Ramaswami files a petition under Section 145 of the Criminal Procedure Code to the effect that Kanniah is disputing his land, and that he fears a breach of the peace and prays for an order of possession. If the Magistrate knows the history of the case he will probably tell Ramaswami to go to the devil; but as he is a First Class Magistrate this time and Ramaswami has so far been dealing with lower orders he most likely does not know and Ramaswami gets his possession order and his second card for the new suit—which he now promptly files. As a matter of fact both his cards are more or less worthless, but they afford him infinite satisfaction in the getting, and help to carry on the game in which his whole heart is immersed. That is part of what is meant by "criminal litigation."

As a result of his all too brief experience of the Indian litigant the Civilian is left wondering on two points. He wonders in the first place whether there is any lower-class Indian family whose members —or sections of whose members—do not hate each other like poison. The books, he is aware, say that the Indian domestic life is very beautiful, and till it is proved to the contrary the Civilian is prepared and anxious to believe that it is; but he finds it a little hard to reconcile this with the petty hates, the schemings and meannesses and nastinesses that come before him. That there exists in India from Kashmir to Tuticorin a single family none of whose members has ever participated in legal proceedings as complainant, accused, plantiff, dependant, pleader or witness, he is ready to deny with oaths. And in the second place he is left wondering whether something cannot be done to scarify and abolish the abominable petition-writer of the bazaar who exploits this misguided passion of simple and ignorant folk—who sends them up with appeals which are utterly untenable, with petitions which are so much waste of paper, who foists off on some poor woman who wants a petition for maintenance a second-hand petition for defamation and sends her off to present it, who deceives and battens and exploits, all for the sake of his few miserable annas. If the Government would sanction in such cases the good old punishment of whipping, the Civilian would be happy to offer them his personal services on the bench for an hour every afternoon.

It occurs to the Civilian, reading over what he has so far written, that a supporter of progress and the Westernizing of India might turn upon him with the good old Morayshire proverb: "Feels and bairns should never see hauf-deen wark." Children, that is, and the feeble-minded should not be permitted to survey processes; for them the completed result only, which alone they can comprehend. India of to-day is very certainly "hauf-deen wark," and perhaps the Civilian lacks the intellect or the experience to see it in the proper light. He is by no means set up with his own judgments—indeed, if you will refer right away back to the Fable of the Contradictory Informants, you will recollect that he has never claimed them as judgments at all. He will therefore admit the implication of the above quoted proverb if his opponent will answer him three questions. Sir, your attention, if you please. "Are you trying to Europeanize India?" "No, most certainly not." "Then are you not endeavouring to guide the Indian to work out his own salvation along European lines, to bring him with only his edges off into the sphere of European society?" "Well—er—yes." "And what are you doing with him when you get him there?" You don't know? Very well, then, the Civilian will tell you a tale.

There is a certain novel called *The Broken Road.* People have said to the Civilian that that is a stupid novel, that it could not happen. The

Civilian will tell them in reply that it has happened, that he has seen it happen. The Civilian's Broken Road was a fool—the Civilian admits it—but he was a good-hearted fool, a kind fool, a merry fool if ever there was one. Europeans in India had borrowed money from his father and gone to dances in his father's house. The Broken Road went to an English University till the money failed and he came back to India and went into the Forests. In the Forests he drank, and under the circumstances the Civilian ventures to predict that most people would have done the same. They took him out of the Forests and put him into another Department and he was a good fool and he pulled up. Then they sent him to a big station and asked the people to be nice to him. The people declined. They would not let him enter their Club. One of them—a clergyman of the Church of England—said that if the Broken Road came into the Club *he* would walk out of it—a truly Christian remark. The Broken Road asked some of them to dinner and they went, and subsequently an American lady among the guests—also, by the way, ecclesiastically associated—said with unction, "My! Isn't he an awful native." Let us look at the Broken Road frankly and fairly; he made Oriental noises with his nose, he talked too much and he laughed too loud, he deviated on occasion from the sobriety and chastity of the righteous; but his manner towards ladies was sound and courteous and the ladies admitted it—and the Civilian thinks that goes for something. He had vices, but so had his critics—the same vices; and he rode keenly and well and he played games gladly—which all of his critics did not. That particular Broken Road is no longer "hauf-deen wark"; the work that was done on him has been done very thoroughly and completely. And a very curious sidelight, too, on the progressive policy in British India. The Civilian will not call this story a Fable nor give it a whimsical title; not that his other Fables are not true, but because he does not think that this is a story which can well be made a joke of at all.

Well, we began with the Lagging Coolie and the Sweeper's Cow and here we are at that finished product, the Broken Road. Without becoming informative—which is the last thing he has any desire to be—the Civilian does not think there is much more that he can say. But just as a last resort he will try to give you a picture of the real and genuine Indigenous, because he has called this chapter "Indigenous," and so far most of the people of whom he has had to write have been only a partially transformed version of that same. Behold then the Indigenous himself. He is an oldish man or at least elderly; for that terrible spirit of "hauf-deen wark" has laid its hold on the younger generation and somehow or other—he admits it is a purely personal whim—the Civilian cannot think of any one under forty-five as really in the class. The Indigenous, then, is an oldish man. He is sitting in his field. He is up to his knees in mud and water. He has broken his plough and he is trying to mend it. He is trying to mend it with a foot or so of rotten rope linked on to a yard and odd of treacherous-looking fibres that he has carefully plaited together, and the whole thing is snarled up with a tangle of cheap string not too new. He has been at it for an hour or two. From time to time he makes kindly noises of expostulation to his ploughing cattle which are wandering at large, he grunts irritably and breaks into snatches of quavering song. He dodders appallingly; he is quite incompetent. He cannot read, he cannot write, he will be very, very slow at taking up anything you may say to him; his eyes are full of a patience that makes light of ages and his face is written over with the long, long struggle of years. He has no clothes and no particular comforts. He will not address you smartly as "Mister" nor sulkily as "Your Honour," nor will he "humbly beg to be excused if he may venture to submit"; he will call you *Babu*, which is "Father," he will say you are his god, he will lay his forehead on your boot, and he will expect you at once to set everything right. He is a poor, stupid, illiterate, incompetent old creature, but after some of the others—oh, how likeable! He does not force himself; he has no intention of taking offence at anything; he will run to get you a coco-nut if you are thirsty; he will carry your gun or beat for you if you hunt; he will follow you everywhere about with a blind and implicit trust that you will do something for him. And of course you do—or you try to—so far as the laws will permit. You are glad to do it, you are anxious to do it—and yet it is hard to say why. He is an old fool—no gainsaying it; perhaps a greedy old fool, perhaps a self-seeking old fool, certainly a uselessly unprogressive old fool; but he is a nice old fool and one likes him. And there are so many, many fools who are not nice and whom one—well, likes less.

May the gods preserve him, and preserve him—Indigenous.

X

IMPORTED

THOSE same novelists of India, for whose vivid gifts the Civilian has ere now expressed his admiration, have not infrequently startled him by the marvellous places they have had the fortune to describe; but the wonder of their places has always been as nothing beside the wonder of their people. This applies of course to all fiction where there is no very deliberate attempt at character-drawing and where—as perhaps it should always be—the play's the thing; but the Civilian is loath to believe that these people of the Indian novelist—he does not think it is necessary to expatiate on the type of novelist he means—are no more than lay figures whereon to drape the remarkable series of incidents that are certainly going to happen. He thinks they must exist.

He wishes to get away to that country of the Indian novelist, to meet these super-Colonels, those charming subalterns, those delightful matrons, those bright and beautiful girls—especially of all, those out-and-out villains. He longs to have to deal with Captain Julian Vavasour of the 400th who made sneering and coarse remarks about Miss Devereux-

Devereux at the Club; he longs to go up to him, knowing him for a real villain, an out-and-outer, and striking him between the eyes say " Take that, you contemptible cur." That would be a grand moment. But in real life he would find that the fellow who had made the objectionable remarks was one of his own friends and at all ordinary times a very decent soul indeed; and the whole thing would be at once horribly complicated. You cannot go up to a member of your Club with whom you have just been playing billiards and strike him between the eyes and call him a contemptible cur—at least, you can, but you are not likely to derive much enjoyment from the process. Oh, sweet imaginary world of coaly blacks and snowy whites, how easy you would be to live in! And how nice to meet these kind and exalted and generous and noble and sweet-tempered people! Well, as the Civilian says, they must exist somewhere; but it is not in Madras.

In descending into cold water it is best to do so at a plunge. Hear, therefore, at the outset the Fable of the Collector and the Junior's Soup. The Collector had come to camp in the Junior's station and as a natural result the Junior was putting him up—and putting up with him—as well as he could. Came the hour of dinner, over which the Junior had taken a good deal of pains; and the boy set the soup upon the table. The Collector tasted it. "Boy," said he, " take this soup away and give it to the dog." The Junior, forbearing as he might be, flushed up a little. " I'm sorry you don't like it, sir," said he. The Collector stared at him. "Good Lord!" said he, " you didn't cook it, did you ? " A sweet exhibition of manners and good taste, say you, my masters ? Even so, but that is not the point of the story. The point of the story is that it was ever afterwards told by the Collector himself with great glee and gusto as an illustration of the absurd touchiness of Juniors in general and this Junior in particular. That, the Civilian thinks, is really fine. He thinks that it brings us from the world of novelists into the realities of life in no uncertain style.

Primarily, the Imported in India must be divided into those who are Sahibs and those who are not—enrolment under these heads of course varying with taste and locality. On the whole the non-Sahibs are the more interesting, but the Civilian must leave them out here because—oh, well, for obvious reasons. And among the Sahibs he wishes to eliminate at once the considerable sub-class of Passengers. Most British regiments are Passengers ; they come out for a year or two, they import with them their own institutions, they do not see much or anything of India and they do not much care if they don't. Globe-trotters also come under this category and Travelling M.P.'s of the harmless order—like Paget ; the designation under which those of the non-harmless order fall the Civilian will beg to be excused from specifying. Under this class, too, fall all Bright Young Girls out for a cold season ; this, of course, is quite natural ; but not so naturally it also embraces a huge aggregation of souls male and female who spend years—possibly decades—in India and contrive to pass through it all with their eyes and their ears hermetically closed. These are the true Passengers, the largest and most infuriating section of that irritating class; they will always tell you they "hate natives" and innocently ask you—you being in charge of ten thousand square miles or so, three hundred miles up-country—how it is that you did not always live in Madras. Or they will ask you why you have to have clerks, or what *abkari* is, or if a Tahsildar and a Havildar are the same thing. . . . And they will generally conduct themselves like idiots, and make things a little more difficult for everybody than they were before.

Contemplating the residue of Sahibs left by the elimination of the Passengers, the Civilian wishes to draw your attention to three great schools or academies of thought. These are the Six Months School, the Cold Water School, and the Mamulites. The Six Months School consists almost solely of ladies and its chief dogma is that the plains of India—any plains of India, irrespective of sea-breezes, greater or lesser comforts, pleasant country or the like—are totally uninhabitable for at least six months of every year; and during the other six months are only made habitable by punkahs, ice, clubs and all the Home papers. They are very nearly Passengers, but they just aren't, and that is where the trouble comes in. A member of this school will tell you that, having been three years married, she has spent eight months with her husband and has only been home once—for eleven months. If to this confidence you should inadvertently reply " Good God ! " or words to that effect, you forfeit her friendship—which is likely to be very charming—for months if not for ever. The correct response is to condole with her, assuring her that to see her wilting in the heat would be infinitely more painful to her husband than any length of separation. So it would ; *but*—there are few districts in Madras where there is unendurable heat for six whole months and none where the cold weather is only sustainable in headquarters. But the Civilian does not like to criticize ladies and so enough of the Six Months School ; at worst they are a small minority that the others make good. But the Cold Water School is important—if only because the Civilian has cited it so frequently in the past. He will now explain more fully what he means by it, and after his manner he will exemplify his point by means of a Fable.

Once the Civilian, posting hard across the face of India on some weighty affair, came to a place where the journey presented some difficulties ; so he called to his side a Tahsildar, which is the correct procedure in such cases, and demanded of him how the thing could be done. " Sir," replied the Tahsildar, " it is utterly impossible. It was never done by any one. It cannot be done." " It must be done," said the Civilian, " or I shall get into most tremendous trouble, and very possibly so will you." " Very well," said the Tahsildar, " I will go and see." " Then," pursued the Civilian, " you do not really know anything about it ? " " No," said the Tahsildar. " Then," cried out the Civilian, " why did you say it was impossible?" But that was a question the Tahsildar could not answer at all. As a matter of fact, however, the answer was very easy; all he had to do was to say "Because I belong to the Cold Water School." But he could not say so, because —poor man—he did not know that he did. It is hardly necessary to say that the Civilian found on investigation that the terrible and impossible journey was a trifle uncomfortable but in reality easy enough.

From the Fable of the Civilian and the Discouraging Tahsildar you are to understand the nature of the Cold Water School. They have never been to see or put any intelligent questions to those who have, but they know instantly that the thing is always impossible, or if not actually impossible so difficult and so unbearable that no sane person would attempt it. They are like the Tahsildar, they do not know that they belong to the Cold Water School, so they can never give you reasons; they just have a vast conviction that it cannot be done. If you have taken to yourself any new toy or trinket and foolishly betray pleasure therein, they will cry out to you that it will not work; if it subsequently is found to work perfectly well or is of such a nature that it does not require to work, they fall back on their reserves and say that it will not last. If you are posted to a new station and are unwise enough to ask their opinion, they will instantly sketch out a picture beside which the Inferno itself were desirable. If you are going out to shoot, they will tell you there is nothing to be shot; or to ride, they will say it is the most dangerous ground in India; or to swim, they will frighten you with bugaboo tales of sharks; or if only for a walk, they will insist that it is going to rain.

You can, of course, get back on the Cold Water School by liking things, by being contented with your place and your possessions, by carrying things triumphantly through without the favour of their advice, and thus you will derive a certain tearful satisfaction from the spectacle of their vast annoyance; but withal they are an extreme weariness to the flesh. Heaven help them, for theirs must be a poor sort of life, but in the latter day may Heaven also remember what a stumbling-block they were in the way of the happiness of others. They are numerous, they are united, they are strong, they are everywhere. Indeed, if the Civilian had not a theory to account for their existence, he would not have the heart to write about them at all. But see his illustration of the Discouraging Tahsildar; it was the sort of thing you would expect from a Tahsildar, was it not, for the Tahsildar was an Oriental and Orientals are not given to striking afield. You could understand the Cold Water School at once if it was a sub-division of Orientals; it only puzzles as a sub-division of Sahibs. Inference, therefore—clear, the Civilian thinks, as day—the Cold Water School is a by-product, if not a symptom, if not a step, in that great, slow-moving but indubitable process, the Orientalization of the English in India. He requests that you will mark this conclusion well, and draw from it such solace as you may.

When we come, as we must come next, to the very

great and powerful sect of the Mamulites, the thing becomes clearer still. Let us consider the cardinal principle of *mamul* and its ingredients. *Mamul* is that attitude of mind which postulates that it is right to do a certain thing in a certain way, that it will always be right to do it in just that way, and that it would never be right to do it in any other way. There need be no obvious reason for doing it in this special way, except, perhaps, that this was how it was first done, and although improvements may have suggested themselves, still, as it was done in the beginning, so it must continue to be done till the end. Now, any one who has dealt much with native servants will be able to tell you that in initiating any new practice—even if it is only some trifle of serving at table or taking certain luggage into camp—you must be most careful, for exactly as it goes on that first occasion so it will go ever after. Once a thing has become a *mamul*, all is thereafter perfectly simple; it will practically do itself, and the maintenance of it in that crystallized and defined state will be a very precious thing to all concerned. Now this is an entirely Oriental view; it is the attitude produced by a country where the passage of epochs leaves hardly a mark and where a thing may be done at this day exactly as it was done a hundred or a thousand years ago. It is certainly not an attitude germane to the English. The English people did not persist in driving in carts after Stephenson had set his train running on its rails, they do not refuse themselves the advantages of the telephone or the electric light or the phonograph or the petrol engine; they are a restless people, they pry out and adapt and pry out further again. But in India—or in that part of India of which the Civilian has been speaking—your Sahib is more of a Mamulite than the native himself. He regulates his life by it, he punctuates his career with stereotyped incidents—going home, buying a motor-car, getting married—which must occur at the scheduled time and at no other stage thereof; he takes his day in a fixed and unalterable order. He regards certain things as right to do and certain others as wrong and there are no other classes of things but these. It is *mamul* to go to the Club in the evening, to ride before breakfast, to have mulligatawny soup at tiffin on Sundays, to dine about nine o'clock and to go to bed immediately afterwards; it is *mamul* to be cheated by one's servants and to allow one's peons to do no work, and the *mamul* attitude towards these defaulters is not of anger but rather that of one who watches a highly amusing comedy. It is *mamul* to put up with almost anything, and to discourage with severity all attempts to break off into original ground. It is *mamul,* in a word, to be *mamul.* Now this is the cardinal principle on which the Orient has run itself since it first swam into the ken and observation of Western humanity—and probably long before.

Let us now quite frankly and as a possibility view the Orientalization of the English in India. The Civilian has already laid before you the consideration of the Cold Water School and the Mamulites and we have studied them together for what they are worth. He does not intend to bore and insist, for the insistent bore is a most shocking creature altogether, but in justice to the great principle of the Orientalization of the English in India he is compelled to lay before you two further aspects. Having done this he will expatiate no more and will leave you to your own considerations. Each aspect he will introduce by a Fable. The first shall be the Fable of the Segregated Females, and the second the Fable of the Amusements Committee.

One evening the Civilian went to a garden party, and to this garden party many progressive Indian gentlemen came bringing their wives. They set the wives down all together on a row of chairs in the background where their *saris* made a most glorious rainbow of colour, and there they left them and no one took any further notice of them. When it was time to go they collected them and took them away. The wives expected nothing else, they were perfectly happy, they said nothing, they did nothing and they got nothing, but it was all delightfully *mamul* and correct. . . . The next evening the Civilian went to the English Club. He there saw that his friends came and brought their wives, took them to a part of the building set apart for their use, set them upon chairs among other wives, conceded them a glass of lemonade and then went away at once to the billiard-room. There they remained so long as the spirit moved them, and when it moved them no longer back they came, called the carriage, singled out their particular wife from among the patiently waiting group and took her away. The wives had sat there together all the evening talking about servants and had lived over again every single household worry of the day; they had stood each other plain sodas and glasses of lemonade and plates of potato chips, but no male came near them or attempted to show them the least attention in any way. The Civilian went to try and speak to them, but he found it was so unexpected and so un*mamul* that it only made them a little uncomfortable, so he went away quickly seeing he had blundered. Between the conduct of the Indian gentlemen and ladies at the garden party and that of the English ladies and gentlemen at the Club there was no really appreciable point of difference, and in both cases the ladies thought it was all right and expected nothing more.

Now for the Amusements Committee. The Amusements Committee pursued its career of usefulness in a hill station, so whatever you blame you cannot blame the poor Climate this time. It was proposed to hold a concert at the Club at six in the evening, and the Civilian, whose days in the land were not then very long, suggested that six was an awkward sort of hour and surely nine would be better. "Why not," said he, "have it at nine?" "Because, my dear sir," said the Chairman of the Committee, "we should not get one single soul to turn out. If you want after-dinner shows you'd better get back to town. It's not done in Madras. Sensible people, after dinner, go to bed, they don't go to concerts." The feeling of the meeting was evidently with him and the Civilian said no more;

but he thought and his thoughts--which had already perhaps been running a little upon the Orientalization theory—took some such form as this. Ethnologists are agreed that *mamuls* as to meals are only less indicative than *mamuls* as to sex. Further, European and Indian are alike rightly agreed that the most important event of the day is the evening meal. Well and good; but how differently do the East and the West view this supreme function. In the West it is a prelude—you do not, that is to say, go to the theatre first and then dine afterwards; in the East it is the finale and after it there is nothing left but bed. Our ancestors dined and then drank; the East drinks and then dines: final again. Now this last was the view taken by the Amusements Committee in the Fable, and it is the view taken by the majority of those Englishmen with whom the Civilian in his wanderings has come in contact. The day's work or amusement being done, he does not then, after the proper custom of his forefathers, sit down to dinner at six or seven; instead he goes to the Club. After dark, when neither tennis nor riding nor any other pursuit can be keeping him out, you will find him adjourning to the billiard-room, and there he will remain till nine or half-past having all the drinks he intends to have that night. Then home, dinner, bed in rapid succession. It is the very spirit of the East, and if there be anything in ethnology then we shall all be Orientals very soon. The Civilian cannot blame the gods of Hind for dealing thus with his compatriots, for the gods of Hind are very great; but he does think it a slightly cynical jest on their part to imbue those very men whose footsteps they are hastening towards Orientalism with the misguided hallucination that they are Westernizing India.

"Well, Civilian, you have divided your Sahibs into Passengers and Mamulites—for the Six Months School and the Cold Water School seem really a graded kind of Passenger. Is this exhaustive?" Far from it; but not Buffon nor Linnæus himself could carry the classification much further. Heaven forbid that the Civilian should portray you a Presidency peopled solely by Passengers and Mamulites; that would be Benighted indeed. But the others, he fears, must just remain—the others. Remember Captain Julian Vavasour and how in real life all blacks and whites tend to become grey. Already our classifications are beginning to overlap, and if the Civilian went much further he would be constrained to embellish his work with diagrams like the charts of geological strata. Moreover, to gibe at faults is easy and entertaining; to exhibit good examples agreeably is neither. So just take it from the Civilian that the others *are* there—and give thanks for it as he does.

Once upon a time—to change the subject—the Civilian inquired of three ladies recently arrived in India what it was in this country that had struck them most. He asked them separately so that there might be no risk of collusion. The first lady said that she had been by far the most vividly impressed by the mosquitoes—thereby, as the Civilian fears, jesting with him and fobbing off his earnest desire for truth. The other two said that what had struck them most was the extraordinary lack of rudimentary manners in the men they met. These were their words: "The extraordinary lack of rudimentary manners." For this the Civilian was by no means unprepared; he had noticed it himself. At home ladies tend to be sought after, tend to be petted and protected, tend to have little attentions showered upon them, tend to be deferred to, amused, noticed. In India nobody takes any particular heed of them at all; men do not mean to be rude, but whether it be through living too much in the backwoods with nothing but camp furniture or whether it be only the good old Climate again, there is no doubt that they are very often most shockingly mannerless. The Civilian has seen a lady call her own carriage—and the Indian servant, remember, does not hasten when called by ladies—while a young loafer sprawled in a long chair five yards away; he has seen a lady rise and put down her own glass while the man she was talking to did not budge; he has seen—oh, he has seen the most amazing gaucheries. And the Civilian, mark you, is no stickler for punctilio at that.

One weary day the Civilian and Mrs. Civilian were having lunch with a Collector, and three Divisional Officers came to lunch too. Mrs. Civilian had to come in to lunch—though she knew what it would be—because she was staying in the Collector's house, and it is also to be noted that the Collector and the Divisional Officers had been talking shop steadily for three hours in the office.

The Civilian just wondered if they would knock off for the period of lunch. They didn't. They talked on steadily round and across Mrs. Civilian about their drains and their ditches, their schools and their hospitals, their clerks and their Tahsildars and their Taluk Board Members—all of which, of course, was to that unfortunate lady so much gibberish or Greek. When they touched momentarily on the Civilian's own Division she did indeed understand and might have spoken, but she well knew that if she displayed any acquaintance or interest it would be said instantly that she was attempting to run the Division. (This may appear to you incredible, but it is none the less what would certainly have happened.) So she ate her tiffin *plurima volvens*. Now, as the Civilian has said, Mrs. Civilian was an old hand at this sort of thing and it was only what she had learned to expect, but think, please, how it would all have appeared to a young lady, a bride, let us say, fresh from England, who had put on a nice frock for the occasion out of her trousseau and had ventured to think she might be an object of some interest to her fellows. Good for her? My dear sir, you talk like a fool; disappointment was never yet good for any one, and Heaven knows that is a commodity which in India does not require to be manufactured. Side on her part? Bosh! no more side than it is side for a bird to have pretty feathers and to sit in the sun where they can be seen. Why couldn't she take an interest in the conversation? Sir, on the day that you take a bright and comprehending interest in the

Stock Exchange slang of two brokers in your carriage, or fail to be bored by a technical and terminological lecture on, say, ballistics or etiology, on that day the Civilian will tell you.

"But, Civilian, if, as you have been at pains to assure us, the life domestic preponderates tremendously in your part of the world and all your ladies are safely married and matrons, surely it is a good thing that there should not be too much promiscuous intercourse, too many—er—affairs." Sir, you have a mind like a Member of the Legislative Council. Who ever suggested such a thing? The Civilian thought he had long since disposed of the Plain Tale question and that we had agreed that, in the climate of Madras, Plain Tales simply could not occur. The Civilian gives you his word of honour as a Civilian that he has no desire whatever that they should. He was once in a small station where there was a Plain Tale—it was so Plain that it was almost ugly—and where every one knew all about it except the wretched Mrs. Lothario; and he would not go through those evenings at the Club again, not for ten thousand a month and a house at Ooty. Nay, nay, let us abjure Plain Tales and all their attendant devils as the foul fiend Apollyon himself. All the Civilian asks is a little more courtesy, a little more consideration, a less Orientalized attitude towards the ladies who are among us, a little less taking them for granted and treating them like blocks of wood. After all, they have a good deal to endure and they would be pleased with a little attention now and then and it needn't delay the snooker more than twenty minutes. The Civilian thinks—they will hate him for this, mark you—they would be really grateful. "Then why don't they say so?" Well, *would* they?

The Civilian often wonders why English ladies come to India at all; and he sometimes is tempted to reflect whether it would not have been a good thing if they had, from the beginning, refrained. They have certainly complicated life, and at times, on the question of what they are pleased to term "natives," they can be amazingly uncomprehending and tactless. Again, might not the Vansuythen system of friendliness be achievable in a community of males? Would men alone evolve and elaborate those intolerable nuisances, Station Rows? Well, would they? Is perpetual scandal an improvement on perpetual shop? Read any book of travel or administration in the days before English ladies were, and you will see what the Civilian means when he says they have complicated life. It is true that the men who whitewashed the Vellore temple, who slept in their palanquins with their snoring coolies almost contiguous, who shared their curry—as one such gentleman records—with Armenian traders they met on the way and learned a little from these same Armenians in return, it is true that these were rough fellows and little sensitive; but if they had been as we to-day, had been able to appreciate beautiful carving in stone, had demanded an English bed and silence to sleep in, had considered sitting at meat with Armenians undesirable, then, the Civilian will suggest, they would not have got very far nor achieved nearly so much as they did. And these old fellows knew the people, they were—to use the dear phrase of Government—" in touch with local conditions," as we shall probably never be. These are deep matters, however, and involve at every turn questions of relative values on which the Civilian feels sure that his views would be unsound and unacceptable. So he is not going to bother about them any more.

But he must pause for an instant to reflect upon the curious phenomena of the Matrimonial Illusions. There are two of these. X, let us say, is an unmarried man and lives mostly in the billiard-room of the Club; he is forty-one; he is bald or so nearly so as to be worse; he has one eye; a large and offensive nose—in fact, a snout—bad teeth and a beard. There comes out from England, to spend a cold season with her married sister, Miss Y, who is twenty; who has nice clothes and dainty ways; who is prettily pleased at being in a new country and is thinking, really, of very little else. You could not, if you tried with *mantrams*, if you strove with prayer and fasting, with simples and with holy water, persuade X that Miss Y has not designs upon his person and purse—X, that atrocity, that caricature, that bore, that blot. You might reason with him for hours, you might get him to look in a mirror, you might get a great painter to paint his picture and show it him; and still you would leave him unconvinced. He calls Miss Y a " Man-eater " and thinks himself very smart therefor; he makes offensive bets about her in the billiard-room; he warns and insinuates with hoggish hints and Yahoo jests; he makes a perfect beast of himself. And Miss Y is probably unaware of his existence, or if she has met him at all has shuddered slightly and tried to be kind to him to make up for the terrible unkindness of nature. . . . That is the first Matrimonial Illusion—that all girls who ever came out from home came out for the sole purpose of attracting some such creature as X, "hooking him," if you please. It is a trifle objectionable intrinsically; and there is also the possibility that X and his like with their sneers and their wallowings may put off some one with whom Miss Y had a chance of happiness. "But there, Civilian, you give yourself and Miss Y away; you admit by that that she wants to get married." Surely! The woman isn't a nun. If you cannot see the elementary difference between these things, then you are just as bad as X and the Civilian has no patience with you at all.

The second Matrimonial Illusion is more amusing and more agreeable to contemplate, not being confined to such as X. It consists in the belief that in all married European households in India one of two conditions prevails—either the man is a wife-beater or the woman henpecks. You may think the Civilian is making too much of things, that he is going in for a far-fetched jest this time, but upon his honour he is not and it is indeed so. As soon as he has saved up a little money he intends to take leave and collect Presidency statistics on the subject and then he will convince you. At present, running over all the married couples whom he has heard discussed—and in India if you sit long enough by the throne every one you know will in time come up for judgment—he cannot remember a single one in which one or other of these conditions was not held to exist. A is a Collector; it is nothing but common knowledge that the man cannot call his soul his own, that Mrs. A runs the entire district and that poor old A—not a bad chap really if that woman would only give him a chance—simply does as he is ordered and has to look pleasant over it too. B, on the other hand, is in the Police, and that poor little thing Mrs. B, of course he beats her almost weekly—yes, literally, with a stick. *Seu quid ineptius!* But if you do not believe the Civilian, wait for the statistics.

If you will now be so good as to cast back to the end of what the Civilian was saying about Places, you will find out that you are still, in theory at least, deposited celestially upon the Hills and that there all this discourse about People has taken place. If the Civilian be not mistaken it must by now be near evening and high time we betook ourselves from these foolish altitudes to the Club or some such sensible place. It is, indeed, possible that you may have quietly slipped away already and the Civilian, babbling along merrily, has never noticed. No matter; if you are pleased, so is he. In any case you will recollect that the poet Catullus contracted a severe cold through the writings of some doleful historian—the unfortunate Volusius if the Civilian remembers aright—and had to cure it with an infusion of nettles, which sounds abominable; and lest this should happen to you, and you should subsequently refer to the Civilian as Catullus subsequently referred to Volusius, he thinks his discourse had better draw to an end. A certain friend of the Civilian's once said of a lecture, "A less informative discourse I never heard—nor a more enlightening," and that is what the Civilian would like you to say about him; but even if you cannot—as is indeed most likely—rise to the second part of the antithesis, he still hopes you will be able to allow him the first. He would like also, in a word or two, to make the peace lest there be some who will take him amiss. You, sirs, whose arms are strong and whose heads are wise to control the destinies of many, and who rule and labour and preserve and build and administer and get little thanks for it from any one; and you, mesdames, who have submitted yourselves to this most ungallant of countries from no apparent cause but sheer excellence of spirit; let us at least be thankful that we can laugh at ourselves for then we are the less likely to be laughed at by others. And if at times the Civilian has appeared to be snappish and disagreeable, remember that he is an embittered old man; and if at times he has seemed too eager to reform, too unsympathetic to existing things, remember he is an enthusiastic young idiot; and if at times he has simply appeared preposterous, try to believe that is probably what he meant to be. No doubt India would be a nicer place if there were nobody in it but oneself or oneselves; but as we have all arrived upon its shores several thousands of years too late for any such consummation, let us try to make the best of it, avoiding the sad doctrines of the Six Months School, and say that we are very pleased with it as it is—all of it, that is, except the Cold Water School and the Matrimonial Illusionists. For indeed with these exceptions and perhaps one or two more it is not really so bad as it might be—not, considering all things, nearly so bad as we and our like might have made it, not so bad as we certainly should have made it if some good genius in the place had not stood by and given us a helping hand. The gods of Hind are many, and some few of them are kind. And, after all, you know, the sundial is probably in the right of it. *Horas non numero nisi serenas.*

A number of people—mostly ladies—have said to the Civilian at various times, "Now, look here, Civilian, do you really mean this or are you getting at us in some way?" The Civilian always found this a very hard question to answer because he was never quite sure whether he had meant it or not himself. And if you were now to put it to him with regard to what he has written in this book, he would find the answer more difficult perhaps than ever before.

EPILOGUE

"WELL," said the Superior when he had read what the Civilian had written, "I don't think much of this stuff. I don't follow your descriptions. They aren't the real India at all."

"I never said they were," replied the Civilian. "Indeed, I have been at pains to point out that they are only meant to convey how things appeared to me. Hence the title of this work."

The Superior snorted.

"There's nothing in it," said he. "Do you suppose you're the only man who ever went out after a tiger or saw a paddy-field or did a houseboat camp?"

"No," said the Civilian patiently. "But then, you see, at home and elsewhere, there are a number of people who never did even these ordinary things or ever are likely to. I put in these bits for them."

"And what you say about People," went on the Superior, "is simply pique and ill-temper. You're simply trying to get your own back by annoying them."

"And yet I have tried to make it plain," said the Civilian meekly, "that this last was what I most desired to avoid."

"Huh!" said the Superior graciously and muttered something about a Mission to Instruct, at which the Civilian merely sighed.

"And besides," said the Superior suddenly, "you're too sidey, young man. Calling yourself The Civilian! People won't like that. It's sidey. It'll annoy them. It's uppish."

"Thank you," said the Civilian, "I shall have that bit in. And I am not at all sure that you have not made the most diverting remark in the book."

THE END